Prayer Conversations

By Tammie Gibson and Cathy Mantua

Cathy was diagnosed with cancer in 2020. Things seemed bleak and scary. I (Tammie) had moved several years before and now live states away. I felt helpless. There was nothing I could do to help my friend. I couldn't visit and be present with her. I couldn't offer help with food or driving to doctor appointments. I was at a loss at what to do.

Then God spoke to my heart. Pray. Well, I am already praying, I said. No, text her your prayers.
So I did. Irregular at first, but then decided to be more intentional about it. I set the calendar alarm on my phone to remind me each day to text my dear friend a prayer. I didn't (and still don't) plan any of the words I type into my phone each day to send to her. I just sent words of praise to our God and blessings to my friend in hopes that they would in some way bring comfort and peace.

What you have on the following pages are those texts and Cathy's responses and prayers as she could send them. We shared our burdens and prayed for and with each other along the way. Prayer conversations. They have become a natural part of my daily routine. They have become a source of peace for Cathy and her family, so she tells me. Cathy asked me to put them into a book in hopes that others might find some of what she found in these rather simple prayers. And to honor my friend, I said yes to that assignment and pressed into it with all my heart.

For my Friend:

Cathy, I bet you didn't think you would get any credit, did you? But, we both know that our great and marvelous God gets all the credit. You, lady, are an inspiration to me, of how to walk in faith when on a most difficult, dark journey. Thank you for encouraging me to step out in faith everyday. So, Cathy, here you go. Here is your book of prayer conversations.

Much love,
Tammie

Praying.
Lord, You are in TOTAL control. I ask You to bring continued peace and rest. Hold Cathy close and tight to You. Relieve any all anxiety. Guide the testers. Bring healing beyond medical comprehension. In Jesus name. Amen

> Thank you so much sister! It comforts me to know that I have you praying for me!

You are loved!

> You too dear Tammie!

Dear friend, I pray: God continue to hold Cathy close to you and heal her body. Release the inflammation and heal any and all damage that may have been done. In Jesus name. Amen

I pray that our great God bestow great peace upon you. That the doctors and technicians be skilled and gentle. That the test results be favorable. That you, Cathy, find rest and healing. In Jesus name. Amen.

> Thank you Tammie! This is quite a journey

I'm sure it is.

Lord, bring peace to the anxiousness about tomorrow and the anesthesia. We trust You Lord for all that will happen tomorrow. Take control of Cathy's body and reactions to the medications and procedure. Give her Your peace right now and let nothing else disturb that in her. Thank You for all that You ate working out in her life and the lives of her family. In Jesus name, Amen.

> Thank you so very much Tammie! I treasure your prayers and our friendship.

Me too.

Dear Lord, Cathy is Your child. You have her held tightly to Yourself. Nothing that happens can take her from You. I ask that right now you surround her with Your great love in every form that she needs tight now. Start a healing in her body in a way that only You can. Surround her family with Your peace and strength. In Jesus name, Amen!

> Thank you Tammie

Ps. 62:5-8 (The Passion Translation)
God's glory is all around me! His wrap-around presence is all I need, for the Lord is my Savior, my hero, and my life-giving strength.

Our Great Father, who reigns in heaven and over all the earth, we worship You. You will above all else we truly desire and pray. I ask this moment that You Lord God, would begin to do what is needed in my sister Cathy body, a mutation is needed. You know that right well. We trust in You to do what is best for Cathy and her family, for Your glory. Forgive us Lord of any attitude that is outside Your will. We are but mere humans and afraid and sad. Bring Your peace, dear Lord. Let us not sin against You or be tempted to turn against You. In our small understanding, give us and the doctors wisdom. Light the right path and let it be followed in boldness, heads held high because of our position as Your daughters and sons. In all of this I pray You be glorified and honored. Let Your peace reign. In Jesus name. Amen.

> Tammie. This prayer is awesome. Straightened out my thinking. I was so scared yesterday. If I do nothing I only have a couple months. If it is the mutation, I have an average of 7 years. If it is not the mutation, time will be less and I would have to have chemo. Due to my other problems, immunotherapy (the best treatment) is not an option. My boys are here. I appreciate these prayers via text more than I can express. If I stop responding, I will be reading them as long as I can. After that, Mike will read them and pray them with me. We just discussed this. Thanks so much !!'
>
> Actually, when we prayed as a family, we prayed Gods will for sure.

I know that this has been your heart prayer all along.

Lord, at the end of this day, I pray for deep rest Cathy, Mike, Mark and Scott. In Jesus name. Amen.

Absolutely! God, bless Cathy and family with Your safety and strength. Bring wisdom as they come together to study Your holy Word. Continue bringing blessings in this entire process. Let them all fully rejoice in You this weekend. In Jesus name. Amen.

Lord, we are grateful for a new day. For the sun and the crisp air of autumn. For the sounds that surround us. For the family beside us. For all You have see fit to bless us with on this day, in this moment. We thank You. We rest in Your provision. Today we embrace the simple things that we sometimes neglect to see, hear, smell and touch. We realize how blessed we are to be Your sons and daughters, and we are humbled. Accept our praise, Lord God, and help us to be ever mindful of You in each and every moment today.
I ask Lord that You bless Cathy's time with family and friends. May this difficult time be a time of fruitful planting of Your love and grace into each

of her boys. May they seek You wholeheartedly and bless Cathy with her hearts desire to see them walk closely with You. I ask these things, and give You praises, in Jesus name. Amen.

Lord, bless family time. Bless family members. Give strength and peace. Bring rest and rejoicing. Thank You God for all you have done, all You are doing, and what You are preparing to do in Cathy's life. Let Your light continually shine through her. In Jesus name. Amen

Thank You Lord for Your strength and a new day to experience Your greatness. Bless Cathy and family with views of Your creativity today, in nature and in each other. Continue to be their Peace and Joy as they walk with You on this path. Draw the Mark and Scott to Your heart. Stir Your Spirit within them to desire You, to long to walk close to You. In Jesus Name. Amen.

> Need these at night. Mike is praying your prayers aloud to us. So meaningful. He just read this one in the way to a walk. So appropriate. If you see any short materials on how to die well as a Christian in the final days I would appreciate it. I see books but they are long. Thanks again for the prayers.

I will pray and see where God leads on some shorter things on that topic for you.

My answer is that you are already doing that.

I have listened to these 4 messages and think they will be useful to all of you. Well except for the 3rd, but it still had good stuff.
https://sermons.faithlife.com/series/27243-dying-well-grieving-well

> Thanks Tammie. You are the best!!!!!!!!!

No I'm not. For sure. It is God. All him. I cried when you asked me to find these things for you. And I'm still looking and will send me as God brings them up.
I am highly honored at your request and the way you have accepted my simple prayers for you. Homered that I can have a small part of your journey.

> I will pray for you too Tammie. Thank you so much!

Thank you.

Lord, this day is such a gift from You. Let us not forget that You cared enough for us to create it. Well before you put everything into its place in the universe You created, You knew we would be in this day. You didn't throw in the towel and just not create it all. You could have. I would have, knowing what a mess we would make of things. But You saw Cathy and said, she is worth it. You saw that she would fall in love with You, and that made it all worth while. Would You bring comfort to her and Mike and Mark and Scott in this difficult time? Fro when You saw Cathy, You saw them too, and said that they were worth Your creation, and Calvary. Jesus You understand far better than any of us what is happening. Be their peace that passes all understanding. In the might name of Jesus, I ask that You bring Your healing touch to each mind, spirit, and body according to Your will. Amen

Lord, this afternoon, I am reminded of Your promise and truth that You ARE here in the very center of all we go through. I am making a choice to believe that and hold tight to it. I am not alone. Cathy is not alone. Your live richly flows through her to those around her. Sustain her by Your ever, always, powerful, grace. In Jesus name. Amen.

Merciful Father, as the season changes outside, I realize that You put them into motion right from the beginning. You had the colors and smells and sounds of each season prepared for our enjoyment and understanding of Your majesty. You God are in control. You God deserve our praise. Even when it is hard, both of these things are true and will remain true for eternity.
I don't understand why the life we have here on earth gets hard and painful. But I know You are True and Faithful. Help us rest on that this day. Give us the strength to hold onto You. In Jesus name. Amen,

> Mike and I are praying this right now. Thank God for this ministry of yours

God is good! You are very welcome.

God, I don't know what tomorrow holds, or even the rest of this day. But I know that You hold it and me in Your hands, and that is enough.
Thank You God for holding Cathy, Mike, Mark, and Scott in Your hands. Let them rest all their cares in You. Grant them peace in overflowing abundance as they walk this difficult path. Give them an overwhelming sense of Your presence as they await test rests, treatments, and more test. Through all of this, let Your glory shine. In Jesus name. Amen.

You have no idea how much sending these has helped me over the past weeks!

> Back at you!!!!!

Lord, this is a day we set aside to rest and reflect. Let us rest in You and reflect upon Your goodness to us. Let us rejoice in the now that we have in You. You ARE our God. We lift You up. We glorify Your name. Grant us Your peace through this day. In Jesus name. Amen.

Sunday from Tammie. Lord, this is a day we set aside to rest and reflect. Let us rest in You and reflect upon Your goodness to us. Let us rejoice in the now that we have in You. You ARE our God. We lift You up. We glorify Your name. Grant us Your peace through this day. In Jesus name. Amen.

Sorry. I was trying to send that to the boys. We are praying together. They are sending me Amens and very encouraging comments.

No problem. Sometimes I need my own prayers too.

Father in heaven, thank You for Your steadfastness. When everything around us seems to change and our plans fall through and what is expected to happen doesn't, You are the Rock that we anchor to. You don't change. Your promises are always true. You are truth. Help us to hold tight to the Anchor of Your love and care. Cathy's life is in turbulent water right now. But You Lord God are the Anchor that holds her. Make Your peace known today in her, in Mike, in Mark, and in Scott. Let that peace be enough to hold them fast to you today. In Jesus name. Amen.

Thank you God for the answers you provide and are providing today. Please God make things clear to all involved in Cathy's life and treatment. Be with each person and bless them with Your mighty presence. That's all we really need. In Jesus name. Amen.

Lord God, we lift up our praises to You this moment for the medical results of today, for the hope that they bring. Continue Your healing work in Cathy's body. In Jesus name. Amen!

Lord, today I ask that You help us to rest in Your presence. After a day of seeing Your mighty hand at work and Your moving, we rejoice and rest in You. Though there is rough road ahead yet still, we see Your hands at work to continue to smooth the way or carry Cathy through. Either way Lord You ARE in it, and we place our trust in You again for another day. Hear our prayers for healing. Cleanse our hearts to enable us to hear from You. Most of all God, give Cathy, Mike, Mark, and Scott, You. In Jesus name. Amen.

Father, help us keep our eyes on You. Life swirls around us and we feel like we are all alone, but You are right here holding us close to You. Help Cathy to keep her eyes totally fixed on You and not the medical stuff swirling all around her. Help her to keep her eyes fixed upon Yours. You are the Rock and Foundation of her life, let her rest in that today. In Jesus name. Amen.

Good morning, God. You have painted some wonderful colors among the trees and flowers and it brings joy to our hearts to see Your creativity. Thank You for thinking of Cathy when You created the earth and all that is in it. Thank You for blessing her family with her smile and laughter. We are a part of Your plan, and are amazed that such a great God would see us, but You do. You see the struggle and the joy. You bless each with Your touch. Give Cathy a special touch from You today. Let her experience You joy of her. Sing sweetly over her and continue to give her peace. In Jesus name. Amen.

God, thank You for the healing power of rest, both physical and spiritual. Resting in Your presence and care brings peace and comfort and healing to the body, mind and soul. Allow Cathy to get the rest she needs physically throughout the day, and through the night. Give her spiritual rest throughout as well. These things come powerfully from You as we place our trust in You. So, I ask these things in Jesus name. Amen.

Lord God, I thank You for the wonderful things You have given. For family and friends. For all the amazing creatures and plant life. For the stars, sun, moon and clouds that cross the sky. Bless this day. Bless Cathy and her family as they worship You. Guide in all they say and do. Show them Your love. In Jesus name. Amen.

> Got this from my son tonight. "I'll share it with roxana and smitty before dinner, we're gonna make some sweet potato sushi rolls. They'll appreciate the part about the creatures and plant life, fall has been beautiful, and we just had a friendly bear visit "

That is so cool. Thank you.

Bear visits are neat as long as your inside and their outside.

> This is a miracle for me. Certainly answered prayer. Thank you Lord Jesus! Thanks you so much for sending these prayers. Mike and I went to Ocean City Maryland Thursday through Saturday. It was awesome to be at the ocean. We had a good time. Repeat bronchoscopy is the 16th. Looking for the gene fusion or mutation again. Didn't get enough cancer cells before.

I'm glad you got to get away for some peace and rest. That is a blessing for sure. I'm happy that I can pray for you in this way and time.

> I am happy too Tammie. God did provide you with a very wonderful ministry. I am very grateful.

You are very welcome.

Lord, there are things in this life that are hard. There are things we don't understand. We don't understand the why of this cancer in Cathy. But we do know You. We know that You are and some days that has to be enough. In those some days, we will continue to praise. You are in all and over all. You have Cathy and her family in Your hands. So we praise You for drawing us to Yourself. We praise You Lord even on this path. Thank You for giving us the opportunity to give You praise. Thank You for You love and care. In Jesus name. Amen.

Lord as we draw to the end of another day, I thank You for being in it. You have painted the trees with color. You put a small chill in the air. The sun shone. All of these remind us of You and You care for us. Thank You. Keep Cathy, Mike, Mark and Scott ever close to Your heart and give them the rest that they need to experience another day upon the next sunrise. In Jesus name. Amen.

God You are amazing! You continue to pursue us day in and day out, wanting not one to be lost eternally. You created us and know us down to the very last tiny particle. You know how each part works . you lived us before we came to You and You love us even when we mess up. Thank You for caring SO much about us that You gave us the gift of Jesus. Help up never forget You in all we do. Bring rest, peace, and joy to Cathy and her entire family. In Jesus name. Amen.

Thank you Lord for another new day. Thank you in advance all the things that are going to do in it for us. I asked that your continued peace continue to rain in Cathy's life and amongst her family. Thank you for her and thank you for your peace in Jesus name amen

    Repeat bronchoscopy was this morning. They got the biopsy. 10-14 business days to got the results. All went well.

    Talked with lots of people around here about Jesus!!!'

That's great! Praying for just right results!

    Yes

    We just prayed this together. Mike thanked God for Tammie. This is a wonderful ministry my friend.

Thank you. It's a blessing to me too.

Bless the name of the Lord our God for His rest and peace. Continue to lead us Father and we will continually praise Your holy name. Amen.

Lord, when we ask, "Where is God in this?", let us listen closely to hear You say, "Right here, my beloved. Right here."
Grant us strength for what lies before us and Your rest and peace in this day. In Jesus name. Amen,

> Not sure if you are still in the prayer chain: Thanks so much. It is extremely comforting to have you ladies in my prayer corner. I am praying for these doctors and technicians doing the radiation today. For precision as Elizabeth said stated, among other things. There was a lot of work from doctors and physicists to pinpoint the brain lesions. Called cyber knife. Chemo class is today. Chemo infusion starts 29th

Thanks for the update.

Lord, thank You for the advances in medical treatments. You are amazing in giving these gifts to us. You God are great and loving, please keep Cathy in Your care. We trust You to do what is best. Guide and direct all the technicians and doctors this week in Cathy's treatments. In Jesus Name. Amen.

You ARE in His hands my friend. Blessings.

> I survived day 1 of radiation. No side effects yet. Thank you Lord!

Yes! And we are going to be equally thankful for your healing as well, my friend.

> That's would be a miracle. Christian oncologist said she can't cure me just keep me going longer since it is in both lung nodes and metastasized to the brain. Can't take it out.

Our God is greater!
Ultimate healing IS on the way. It will be sad for those left behind, but you will be healed! That's a harder healing to accept this side of life, I know, but our God will be with you and your family each and every step. Hold fast, my friend.

Lord, You know the path ahead for Cathy. We know that You are able to remove the cancer. We ask that this would be something that You would do for her. But if You choose not to, we will still choose to glorify and praise You. Your will be done. In Jesus name. Amen.

> Ultimate healing!!!! I am actually so happy thinking about that. I am extremely thankful that I did the Revelation study and all BSF studies. Thankful that God made them available and that I was blessed to be included.
>
> Spent day 2 of radiation wrapped in Jesus arms. Prayed the whole time. time flew by. It was almost 2 hours.

God IS so good! Blessings upon blessings to you.

Lord, as always You know what is best and are doing that for Cathy. Continue to be her strength. Give her Your rest in this day. Bless her with reminders of You. In Jesus name Amen

Father, help us remember today that You ARE in complete control! Nothing surprises You. Nothing scares You. Open our hearts to Your rest and peace. In Jesus name. Amen.

> Thanks Tammie! Sitting in radiation now waiting for treatment 4.

Lord, thank You that this week of treatment is complete. Your light shine through in some special ways too. Thank You for that. Thank You for the rest that is now happening and the healing of the body. Thank You for the medical technology that allows things to be so precise.
Be with Cathy, Mike, Mark and Scott as they move into the next steps You have for them on this healing journey. Be their rest and peace. Be their comfort and joy. In Jesus name I pray these things. Amen.

> Amen. Just prayed this with all the boys. We are in the car on top of the bay bridge.

Blessings!

God, on this day, we worship You. For no other reason than You ARE God. Your are worthy of all our praise and honor. Thank You for the gifts You have freely to us. For salvation, the greatest gift of all, we give thanks. Guide us in all we do and say. Let us fully honor You. In Jesus name. Amen

Lord God of all mercy and grace, flood peace into Cathy, Mike, Mark, and Scott. Let them find You as they seek You. Bless them with Your love as they are guided by You through this struggle. You alone are ever and always with us and faithful. We put our trust in You. In Jesus name. Amen.

Father you are our great hope. God you are who we trust in Had we trust in you to continue to take care of Cathy. Help us to not lose hope help us to continue to trust in you. Thank you that you have everything under your control. Continue to guide the doctors and the treatments. We will give you all the glory and the honor and the praise. And Jesus name Amen

God, our needs are great, but You are greater. Help us hold to that fact tightly in this difficult season. Let us be found faithful in all things when we meet You face to face. You are our hope. Let that hope, along with peace, joy, and love be ever in our hearts and lives. In Jesus name. Amen.

Lord, bless Your name. It is higher than any other. Cover us with Your love and care. Fill us with Your peace and joy. We will ever and always give You praise. Our lives are in Your hands. Bring healing to the body, mind, and spirit of Cathy. Be exactly Who and What she needs. Allow her to rest completely in You. In Jesus name. Amen.

> 1st chemo drug starts in a few minutes. Awesome prayer for today. Thanks

Father, I pray for rest and peace to flood Cathy. As her body takes in the chemo, I ask that You would alleviate all side effects. Let her remain focused on You and her love for You and her family. Cause this process to do what is intended, but Lord God, in a gentle way. Give Cathy Your grace as she continues on with You. In Jesus name. Amen.

Father, in the sunshine or the rain, You are in each breath we breathe. You bring peace in despair. You bring hop in darkness. We trust in You. Guide our hearts and lives. In Jesus name. Amen.

> Thanks Tammie! Just a little nausea and fatigue. The meds they gave me reduced the inflammation I have had for 5 years but I go off that med tomorrow. I am going to talk with the doctor about continuing a maintenance dose of that med. she suggested it earlier.

Praise God! Blessings to you!

At the end of this day of worship I Thank you God. Thank you for your mercies and thank you for your rest worship you and Praise your mighty name. I asked that you would continue to bless and continue to heal. That you would continue to guide and that you would continue to direct. In Christ's most precious and holy name Amen

Lord, bless Cathy today in Your own very special way. You know exactly how she hears from You personally, so speak into her in that unique way.

Fill her with You and You alone. Help her to continue in her treatments with the assurance that You are in complete control. Because You are. You are the Great I AM. You are there in her every now. Bless her I pray. In Jesus name. Amen.

Love you lady!

> You too Miss Tammie! You have been so very helpful to me. I can't thank you enough!

May the God of peace hold you firmly in His hand today as you continue your healing journey. May you feel His love and care as you draw close to Him. Lord, we trust in Your full control in each area of our lives. Let is rest in You and You alone. In Jesus name, I pray. Amen.

Lord, in Cathy and Mike's lives continue to reign supreme. Continue to draw them to each other and to You for the support and strength they need to fight this battle. Draw Mark and Scott into a deeper relationship with You. Give them all Your precious peace as they move through the days ahead with You. In Jesus name. Amen.

So, to give you something to pray about: I will be going to a place in Ohio the 15 thru 21 for some intensive therapy. It is called The Healing Care Center. I am in some desperate need of mental and emotional care and healing. And it's time on my journey to get that. I will have 5 days of 3 hours of counseling and an hour of classroom learning, plus homework. It will be intense to say the least. But I have come to the end of myself and need to find something deeper and more of God in it all too. So pray for me that week. I will keep sending you prayers until you are healed!

> My dear friend Tammie, my heart goes out to you. I have never suffered from depression until now and it is certainly a disease that needs medical treatment. I pray that you can get the help that you need, and it will be effective and long lasting. You've been so faithful to me during my journey and I pray that I can be as faithful in my prayers to you. I will pray for you dear Tammie. I am very sorry that you are going through this. It must be extremely difficult. I do look forward to your return from your trip with a renewed spirit and outlook. You certainly hide it well and I can tell that you have been working in this as hard as you can. May this treatment center be just the extra help you need to recover!

> My next chemo is scheduled for the 18th. We can pray for each other. praying for you Tammie.

Oh, I will be praying for sure. And thank you for praying for me. God has worked this whole thing out with His perfect timing!

God, today is Your wonderful gift to us and we rejoice in it and give You praise for it. Let us find You in all that we encounter and do today. Help us in our weakness to allow You to be strong. You are God and there is none greater. We trust ourselves to Your care on this day. In Jesus name. Amen.

Lord as You give rest and comfort to Cathy, I give You praise for her wonderful example to me and others around her. Thank You for the encouragement she gives in her time of need. Continue to bless her with minimal if any side effect. Be her strength and guide through this entire healing process. In Jesus name. Amen.

> Tammie. I marvel at your support of me during your time of great need yourself. I am praying for you. You are such an encouragement and example to me. I am now listening to an Audible the last book suggestion you emailed to me. It is really helpful. Thanks so very much!

God is good to us both in being able to support each other this way.

> I can't see that I am doing anything for you like you are doing for me, but please let me know if you can think of anything.

Prayer is what I need the most.

God is the only One who can guide me to the level of healing I need and am seeking. So your prayers are very important to me. Thank you.

> Just know that you are very important to me and my family. My boys have a daily prayer which brings us all together. They also see what a true friend is. And the resources your have directed me to with time and research have been invaluable.

You are welcome. If I can do anything more let me know that. God has placed you on my heart.

> Thank you friend. You are on my heart as well.

Lord, bless Cathy's men in their pursuit of You. Guide their hearts and minds to become more and more like Yours. Continue to bless Cathy with these victories and blessings. You are SO good to us. You bring hope in the darkness, EVERY time. Thank You and praise Your name. In

Jesus name. Amen.

Lord God, thank You for the sunshine today. Thank You for Your presence, Your guidance and Your love. You have protected us today from things that we aren't even aware of. Bless Cathy, Mike, Mark and Scott in a special way that can only come from You. In Jesus name. Amen.

On another note: If chipmunks wore underpants the one here would have had to change his. He didn't expect me to be sitting on my swing just a minute ago!

> So happy you could be outside today. It's beautiful here. 75 and not a cloud in the sky Mike and I went on a walk. I am feeling better as is the last two days. How are you Miss Tammie? You are going to be a joy to work with when you get to treatment.

I'm doing well. A bit anxious about the upcoming time in treatment. But God does go before me.

> And will be with you every step.

Yes He will. I am looking forward to victory and healing.

Lord, God, You've got this. You are in control. We are not. So we place our trust fully in You. Keep us ever close to You. In Jesus name. Amen.

Father, bless Cathy with laughter and plenty of it. In Jesus name. Amen.

Lord, You know that some days are more difficult than others. Some days down here there is not and other days pain. But in each, one thing remains constant and sure, You and Your love for us. Wrap Your live around Cathy, Mike, Mark and Scott. Hold them tight. In Jesus name. Amen.

Lord, come close today. Banish all the negative thoughts and attitudes that surround and try to invade. Help us to think on You instead. We love You God and worship You. Thank You. In Jesus name. Amen.

Lord as this day closes, I ask for a refreshing nights sleep and full rest for Cathy and Mike. I ask that they find the deepest rest in You. Bless them and comfort them. Guide them in all they do. In Jesus name. Amen.

> Tammie, I am praying all your prayers for me for my family and yours.
>
> Lord, I thank you for Tammie and how you have created her exactly as you planned and as your creation, she is fearfully and wonderfully made. I pray that as she knows this and feels your loving arms around her and your great love as she enters a healing program. I pray that you enable her to get everything out of the program that you have already planned for her. Please walk with her everyday she is there holding her up, preparing and filling her heart and mind and orchestrating her healing as it is your will. In Jesus name, Amen

Super Amen to that! Thank you.

Dear God, thank You for my friend Cathy. Thank You for Your spirit residing in her. You are the One we worship and praise. You have given us this life and allowed these trials into it to draw us closer to You and to shine Your glory to those around us. Lord, even when we falter, You can shine through. Thank You. Praise Your name. In Jesus name I ask for continued Peace and healing. Amen.

Lord today I thank you for all that you are going to do. I praise your name for keeping up close to you. I asked that you would continue to comfort guide and direct. Father continued to love on Cathy and be her peace Jesus name

Lord as the first day of another week comes to a close, I thank You for Your presence in it. You are very close all the time, continue to allow us to feel that. Knowing You are right beside, before, behind, below, and above brings us comfort, security and peace. Thank You for being available at all times in any place we are in. Knowing that You will be there tomorrow allows us to rest this night. Thank you for being with Cathy, Mike, Mark, and Scott through this entire day. Give them Your rest in this night. In Jesus name. Amen.

My friend, God started working first thing this morning, even before my first session! I have the entire place to myself. No distractions. Just God and me after the 3 hrs of therapy and 1 hour of structure lessons. I have hope. Thanks for praying for me. Please continue. Today was a wild ride of a day and its only day one.

> Lord we praise you for your wisdom and peace. Thanks you for providing what your precious daughter Tammie needed in day 1. We thank you for the progress today and pray you will orchestrate each day according to your perfect will. In Jesus name, Amen.

Thank you!

Lord, as I watch the snow fall outside the window here, I am amazed at Your creativity and the way You surprise me. Continue to bless and honor Cathy and Mike on this difficult road. Draw near to them and help them to see the beauty You have for them even in these difficult days. You are at work even in the darkness. Thank You for Your presence, Your love and peace. Let this time be of great significance to each of them and those that surround the. In Jesus name, I pray these things. Amen.

> 11/17 oncology dr. appt: they got enough information from the last bronchoscopy. I have a Her2 mutation which allows me different IV chemotherapy if I can't handle the ones I am on now. The Her2 mutation targeted chemotherapy may or may not be better than what I am on now, but different. Therefore, I may or may not be able to handle it better. Tomorrow, I will have round two of chemotherapy and they will add Keytruda which may add to the fatigue. They are adding Pepcid for allergic and GI issues and tapering the anti-inflammatory so hopefully I won't have a flare of my other conditions.

God is with you and in this! I will be lifting you up.

Lord, today help Cathy set her face toward You as she undergoes another treatment. Hold her in Your ever loving arms, tightly, close to Your heart. Remove any and all fear. Guide the medical staff in their ministrations to her. Be with Mike as he holds her hand. Continue to give them the strength for just the next step. Radiate Your presence in them, through them, and all around them. Be Mark's and Scott's closest friend in all that they face today. We place Cathy fully in Your gentle hands and ask these things in Jesus name. Amen

> I am praying for you my friend as well. All of this back at you. We are both alone. Mike can't come in due to Covid.

> I am praying your prayer back to you all well as my extras. Mike is praying too.

Thank you. It is a rough start to my day today.

> Oh, I am so sorry!

Just some battles after yesterday's victories

> Imagine Jesus holding your one hand and the rest of us who love and are praying for you, holding the other. You are an amazing woman. Fearfully and

> wonderfully made. You have been instrumentally helpful in my journey. I can only imagine how many others you have helped and planted seeds for along your way!!!

I'm trying. Thank you

Blessings dear sister. Rest in Jesus. He holds your hand just as He holds mine.

> Yes he does. Any better yet today? I know this is hard work. My prayers are with you sister

Better, yes. Learning to hear the places within me that need attention and nurturing.

> Good girl Tammie!

Lord, give Cathy rest of body. These treatment that are to be ultimately helpful to her can be painful and cause sick and yucky things to happen. What she needs most Lord God You know, so we trust You to provide it, whether it be directly from You or through a family member or friend, let it flow freely to her. Lord surround her with peace and quiet and rest and most of all love. Bless her from top to bottom, I pray. In Jesus name. Amen.

> Tammie. Thank you so much. I pray the same for you. Hope you at making good progress today!

I am. I am learning some new skills to put into practice to grow me healthier in every way. I even got to paint a rock today!

God, it's a new day that we get the chance to see You work. I don't know how You are going to show up today, but my eyes and ears are open. Open to see the smallest thing and hear softest whisper. Make me ready in the waiting to shine Your glory wherever and whenever You decide. Give me Your heart to love those you put in my path. Thank You Lord for the fact that on this journey, smooth or rough, You walk beside us. Bless Cathy, Mike, Mark and Scott today with wonderful glimpses of You at work. Because You, Lord, ARE at work, in and around each of them. Softly, gently, ever drawing them close to You. In Jesus name. Amen.

My friend I am filled with, not just a little hope, but a big heart full of hope!

> This is awesome news. Thank you Jesus!

Jesus invites: Come away with me and rest awhile." Rest can be worship.

Mark 6:31

God, You are our strength in time of weakness, and in times of wellness. Thank You that You are so gracious to us. We've done nothing to deserve it, we can never earn it. You simply offer it for us to take and live in. How marvelous You are! Bless this day with Your eyes to see and ears to hear, exactly what You have for us now, and even a glimpse of eternity with You. In Jesus name. Amen.

> How is my friend Tammie today? Praying you are adjusting to being home and using your new tools. Praying you are feeling Jesus arms around you this evening.

I am very good. I'm not home though. I traveled farther north to upstate NY to visit an old college friend for a few days. I didn't feel that I could be emotionally or spiritually safe at home so I planned for time with someone who is. Jesus has me wrapped in His arms for sure!

Lord bless my friend Cathy as she winds down her day. Give her rest and peace, in Jesus name. Amen.

> Glad you are doing well! I am praying for your home situation. Take care Tammie.

Thank you. God is working on that front as well I believe. Blessings.

PRAISE GOD AND HALLELUJAH! HE IS WORKING IN MIGHTY AND POWERFUL WAYS!!!!!
I could just cry with joy in how He is working in my counseling client's life!!!!
I didn't know I could hold any more happy in me until now!

> Thank you Jesus! I am sooo happy for you Tammie!! This makes me so happy too!

I thought it might! Jesus is working!

> Not a surprise about Jesus working

You are right. I'm just surprised at being a part of it.

> Oh I am not surprised at all. Not at all friend.

Thank you. My heart is happy. Deeply happy.

Here's a song for you… New Today by Micah Tyler

Lord help us to remember that Your mercies ARE new today. Bless Cathy with an outpouring of them. Flood her heart and mind and soul and body with You, Your love, Your peace, Your presence. Grant her deepest desire. Let her see with early eyes that which You already see in that desire. All for Your glory! In Jesus name. Amen.

Lord God our hearts are only full because if You, so pour more of You in. Fill us to overflowing. Overflowing thankfulness. Overflowing praise. Overflowing compassion. All for Your glory, not ours, never ours. As we have received grace, let us be gracious. As we have received mercy, help us to be merciful. Let us be peace on order to point those without peace to You, The Prince of Peace. We love You Lord. Bless Cathy will all of the above and so much more. In Jesus name. Amen.

Good morning God. On this Thanksgiving Eve we thank You for all You have provide and are going to provide. We love You Lord and praise Your name. Continue to work in Cathy's body just what is needed. In Jesus name. Amen.

> Praying for you as well dear Tammie. I pray you can see Gods hand working in your life going before you. Happy thanksgiving dear.

Lord thank You for family and friends. Bless Cathy and family tonight with all You have. In Jesus name. Amen.

> Oh Tammie, there is so much to be thankful for!!! for your progress and every day. For Jesus the one and only. With the Lord a day is like a thousand years. Happy thanksgiving friend.

Lord, in this mixed up world we are thankful for You solidness. Help us to stand firmly on You as our foundation. When things are difficult, remind us that You never change. Bless Cathy and Mike with time with You and each other. In Jesus name. Amen.

As another day comes to a close Lord, I thank You for Your peace and rest in it. Even when things may be difficult to do or think about, Your peace and presence make to alright. When we focus on You, then the peace truly passes all understanding on our part. We trust You God to do what is best. Help us to keep following You. In Jesus name. Amen.

Lord, on this first Sunday of the Advent, I thank You for sending You Son that first time. Thank You for this season where we get the opportunity to experience You birth and the hope You brought into the world then and now. As we move through these next weeks, remind us each day of the precious gift of You as a baby in a manger. Remind us of the hope that is ours today. Bless Cathy, Mike, Mark, and Scott with that Hope each day. In Jesus name. Amen.

God, You've done it again. You have given us yet another day to serve and praise You. You have given us Yourself again in this day to stand with us as You move in us in whatever is before us. We can live Your abundant life now, in this day. How amazing are You, God, to seek us out for relationship with You! Thank You for the amazing things You are doing all around us today. Amen.

Good day, God. Actually, every day is good because You created it. Thank You for refreshment of our souls. For the joy of another day with You. Help us to live each moment with abandon. Thank You for Cathy and her faith in You. Give her extra doses of You today. Fill her to overflowing. Give her rest and reassurance. In Jesus name. Amen.

Lord God, flow Your peace on Cathy and Mike. Bless them with a super strong sense of Your presence. Guide them gently through all That Is going on around them. Comfort them with Your love. Bless Mark and Scott with Your love and care. Guide them into a deep relationship with You, one that is unshakable. I ask these things in Jesus name. Amen

God, thank You for You wonderful grace. Let it flow to overflowing in Cathy's life and the lives of Mike, Mark, and Scott. Be ever constant with them. Constant peace. Constant love. Constant joy. Constant hope. Constant You. We love You Lord. In Jesus name. Amen

Lord, give Cathy rest. I ask this in the powerful, almighty name of Your son Jesus. May it be so. Amen.

Father, bless Cathy today with Your extraordinary rest and peace. Gently care for her every need. Bless her husband and sons with a joy that can only come from You. Well up within each of them the unexplainable hope that we have in You, that only comes from You. Bless them all so that they can continue to be a blessing to those around them.
Thank You for my friend Cathy and Your everlasting love for her. In Jesus name I pray. Amen.

Thank You Lord, that You have allowed me to be a part of my sister Cathy's journey with You. Thank You for the blessing of her friendship and encouragement over the years. Lord I look forward to the things we will get to share with each other in the years yet to come, here on this earth and in eternity with You. Bless her today with overwhelming joy. Joy that spills out to everyone she talks with or comes in contact with. Thank You that You have her right where she needs to be right at this moment. We live You God, and praise Your name. In Jesus name I lift these things to You. Amen.

Lord on this second Sunday of Advent, peace is the theme. Peace that only You can provide is true and is wonderful. Often we don't understand it, but we know Who is the Source of that peace, Jesus. So we rejoice in Your peace. Bring peace to Cathy today as she reflects on You and leans into You. You are her Source. In times that we don't understand the things happening to or around us, God, help us hold onto You, our true Source of peace. In Jesus name. Amen.

> Good morning Miss Tammie. Thank you so much for these prayers. I just prayed over them for both of us. I am praying for your new job and new outlook and circumstances. That God is over all and holding you up as you are in this new journey. God has certainly put you here and now to be a blessing to me and I know many others.

Lord God, You have a purpose for everything that You allow to touch our lives. You use the good, the bad, and the ugly, for Your glory in our lives. Some of it, well, honestly, God, most of it, I don't understand and I sometimes struggle with that. I don't understand why cancer touches the lives of people I care about. Why some are healed and others aren't. But what I do understand, albeit in a very limited way, is Your love for each of us. So today God, help us to hold onto the one thing that we understand, the one thing that is eternal and most important, You and Your love for us. Let us anchor in You our soul, body, and mind. Let us rejoice in Your plan, even if we don't fully, or even partly, understand it. Thank You Lord for Cathy and the example she has set and is setting in her life. Grant her peace and rest today as she trusts in You. In Jesus name. Amen.

> Amen. Prayed over this during the pet scan. For you also my dear. Pray you are doing well. Thank you greatly.

I am marvelous. I get waves of giddy every once and a while. Loving it.

Therefore we do not give up. Even though our outer person is being destroyed, our inner person is being renewed day by day.
2 Corinthians 4:16 HCSB

Lord, I pray as our bodies waste away, we find joy and growth inwardly. Bless Cathy with a continued strong inward journey with You. Help her find rest and comfort in You every moment. In Jesus name. Amen.

Father, thank You for hearing our prayers. Thank You for doing such a wonderful thing in stopping the growth of the cancer in Cathy. You are all powerful and almighty. And God, I know that even if You had not done this, Cathy would still trust You and follow You. Please continue to work in her body and rid it of this disease. Hold her tight as she holds onto You. In Jesus name. Amen.

Lord, guide and direct the medical personnel today. Help them see what they need to see. Help them know what they need to know. Bring peace to Cathy and Mike. Keep them safe on their journey. Surround them with You presence and love. In Jesus name. Amen.

> Sent this to my boys earlier: I am still at Memorial Sloan Kettering waiting for lab work. I will update more later, but it seems that everything JHU is doing is good. MSK has the same opinion in everything. They did give me an outside hope that if all goes well and I get the cancer shrunk to just a couple lesions and no new brain lesions, they could radiate a couple remaining lesions. We will know that in a year. Said it would have to be a stable, slow growing cancer, I would have to tolerate chemo. All would have to go right. MSK doctor said that my doctor at JHU is one of the beat in the field!!!! Will know everything on the cutting edge, trials etc.

Praise Go's and pass the chocolate!

God, thank You for such good news in Cathy's life on this part of her journey. Thank You for guiding them to a second opinion and look at things. You have had her on track all along, we know that, but having it spoke into her in this way is an extra dose of grace. Thank You for that. Give her and Mike continued peace and lots of good rest.
In Jesus name. Amen.

> I am at chemo so that is good.

God, thank You for yet another day of Your grace. Thank You for being with Cathy and giving her strength and peace each and every day. Continue to guide and direct her and Mike. Continue to lead the medical team caring for Cathy. Help them all to fully rest in You. In Jesus name, Amen.

Lord as the day closes, I thank You for the gift of Your son. I know we celebrate this special gift each year at this time, but Lord, this year we want to experience it differently. We want to sense more of You and less of us this year. Bless Cathy with a special closeness this Christmas season. Draw her closer to You. In Jesus name. Amen.

Lord God, you have opened a new day for us. Thank You for holding us close. I ask that today You would be a place of rest for Cathy, Mike, Mark, and Scott. A safe place to just stop and breathe in deeply Your holiness, Your love, Yourself. Give strength and wisdom where each is needed. Give patience and gentleness for every encounter they have today. Thank You for what You are doing through the medical profession in killing off the cancer in Cathy. We don't know Your total healing plan, but we trust You, and that is and can be enough. So thank You Father for loving and healing us all in so many ways. In Jesus name. Amen.

God, thank You for Your wonderful gifts to us. Salvation, grace, mercy, eternal life, and so much more. All available to any who ask for it. You are our almighty Provider. Praise Your name. Amen.

Lord, give Cathy Your strength today. Let her know in some wonderful, amazing, way that You are carrying her. Bless her beyond measure. In Jesus name, Amen.

Father, I am grateful today for Your care. You watched over us as we slept. You will watch over us as this day moves forward. You are El Roi, the God who sees me. I love that You see each of us as individuals. Thank You for seeing Cathy. For caring for her and loving her so much. Bless her day. And bless all who are in her life. Give her a sense of Your seeing her today. In Jesus name. Amen.

Lord, when we don't understand, give us Your peace. When we hurt, give us Your presence. When we feel alone, send Your warm embrace. Thank You, for loving us so much. Guide us this day. In Jesus name. Amen.

Prayers for you Miss Tammie

Thanks. Quick update. I tested positive for covid. BUT just have symptoms of a sinus cold. I lost sense of smell last Sunday, so I knew to get tested. God blessed with VERY mild case. I'll be out on parole soon!

My smeller has come back. Cinnamon rolls this morning smelled and tasted great!

So grateful all is well. Such blessings my friend. My sister and her husband had a much harder time with it but made a full recovery thankfully

God is good!

Lord God, thank You for my friend Cathy. For her beautiful smile and gentle laugh. Grace her today with things st smile and laugh about. Help us to remember that You too laughed and smiled when You walked among us, and still do I'm sure. Bless those around Cathy with the sense of the presence of Your Holy Spirit, she carries in her. Thank You for all You have done, all You are doing, and all You will do. Help us remember that You are I AM. In Jesus name, Amen.

> Beautiful prayer Tammie. Thank you so much and I prayed it for you too. Much love today my friend.

Thank you. You are a blessing to me!

Lord, thank you for coming as our Counselor. Gently guiding and directing. Carefully advising and tenderly caring for us each day. Help us to be like this for others as Your representatives with others in our lives. Bless Cathy with Your mighty and wise counsel today. In Jesus name. Amen.

Lord, You were there its the very beginning. You were the actual Word of God creating all things. Then You saw the mess we made of things, and intervened by becoming just like us, weak and human. That amazes me. That You would step away from Your deserved glory to become like us. Just so that relationship could be restored. Thank You for doing that. Allow us to deepen our relationship with You. Help us to be ever grateful for Your coming to us as a little babe. Grant Cathy and extra dose of relationship with You today. In Jesus name. Amen.

Jesus, Thank You for coming as a baby to show us Father Everlasting. For laying Your glory aside to put on human skin instead so that we could get a small glimpse of Father God and His eternal love for us. Come alongside Cathy today as a Supremely Loving Father, who is waiting with open arms and bated breath to hold her in His arms. Thank You Jesus, in Your name I pray, Amen.

2 Corinthians 5:1-10 I read these this am in my devotions and thought of you. This tent we live in is NOT our home. Praise His name! Merry Christmas to you all!

Lord, thank You for Christmas. Thank You for that very first gift You gave. A baby, wrapped in strips of cloth. Such a humble beginning for such a glorious Gift. Thank You for loving us enough to start the redemption process, as we couldn't do it on our own. So on this day as we celebrate and remember, I praise and thank You.
Bless Cathy with extra joy this day. In Jesus name, Amen.

> Praying this for you too my dear!

Merry Christmas Miss Tammie!

Lord, thank You for the many gifts in our lives. Thank You most for the gift of Your Son, Jesus. Without Him we would be lost and alone in the dark. But You, Jesus, came and brought light to the darkness that can be found by all who seek it. You brought a return of relationship and we have the opportunity to never be alone. What wonderful gifts!
Because now that we have You in our lives we can also have a deeper connection with other believers. Thank You for that connection that I can have to Cathy across the miles. Thank You for her and her family. Bless them today with the realization of the precious gifts they have, and can have in each other. In Jesus name. Amen.

Lord, thank You for the deep peace that only You can bring. Thank You that You have all of us under Your care. Thank for how gently You are caring for Cathy during this difficult time. Continue to be her peace. In Jesus name, Amen.

God, it's crispy and cold outside today, but I thank You for the warm clothes I have to wear and the warm house I live in. Most if all God, I thank You for the warmth if Your love that fills me up inside. You are amazing! Thank You for caring for us and loving us. Warm Cathy from the inside as well as from the outside today with Your love and care. In Jesus name. Amen

Father, thank You for this day. For all the minutes in within it. Thank You for keeping us safe and in Your care. Please keep Cathy safe and well rested. Give her the strength that she needs and deep rest this night. In Jesus name. Amen.

Lord, our year is slowly coming to an end. This year has felt long and difficult. But we have learned to lean more on You through it. You use all things for Your glory, and we want to give You glory. Thank You for Your guiding of the medical persons in Cathy's life. Thank You for being her strength each day of this year. And thank You in advance for the strength that You already have prepared for her in this next year. We trust You and will follow You. In Jesus name. Amen.

Lord, thank You for the year that now ends. It has been full of challenge and change, but You have shown Yourself faithful through it all. Bless Cathy and her family with peace and hope in this new coming year of life. Help them to celebrate all the little joys along with the big ones to come. Wrap You holy arms around each of them in all that You have awaiting them. Help them lean greatly into You for another year. In Jesus name. Amen.

Praying the same for you Miss Tammie. How is everything going?

Going very well. Thank you!

> I am so glad and thankful that things are going well!

Lord, Let us give thanks to You for all You are to us today. Praise You for who You are, each and every moment of each and every day. In Jesus name. Amen.

God we are reminded of this in Your Word: "And the effect of righteousness will be peace, and the result of righteousness, quietness and trust forever" (Isa. 32:17).
It is only in You that peace can truly come. And this peace comes from the righteousness that You have given through Your Son. Also coming with the peace is quietness and rest. Thank You for these great gifts. Continue to walk with Cathy in righteousness, peace, quietness and rest. In Your Son, Jesus name. Amen.

Lord as this day draws to a close, I want to thank You for the privilege of worshiping You today. Thank You in advance for the rest that we will obtain tonight. Help us to keep our hearts in tune with Yours. Let the beating of Your heart be heard by our hearts as we rest in You this night. Give Cathy unbelievable rest tonight that comes straight from You.
In Jesus name. Amen.

I read these verses in my devotions this morning. I thought of you and thus am praying this Scripture for you today.
In this way, the testimony about Christ was confirmed among you, so that you do not lack any spiritual gift as you eagerly wait for the revelation of our Lord Jesus Christ. He will also strengthen you to the end, so that you will be blameless in the day of our Lord Jesus Christ. God is faithful; you were called by Him into fellowship with His Son, Jesus Christ our Lord.
1 Corinthians 1:6-9 HCSB

May our God richly bless you this day as you walk with Him. In Jesus name. Amen.

> Dearest Tammie, I am praying these verses and prayers for you as well. It is amazing that when you text your prayers about things, they are just at the right time. When you talk about walking with Jesus, I am out walking and singing hymns. When you talk about cold temperatures, I am about to go out in the cold. When you talk about getting rest at night. I am really in need of rest that night having to get up early in the morning for an Appointment. God is certainly placing the appropriate themes on your heart for each

day. Again, please don't feel that you need to send a prayer every day, I can always pray the same prayer days in a row. you could just text "ditto" And I will know you're thinking of me, much love, Cathy.

I love that God is using my prayers. Bless you my friend.

Lord, bless friend Cathy. Guide her in all the decisions and ways she is to go. Thank You for how she blesses those she comes in contact with. In Jesus name. Amen.

Father, today strength was needed, You supplied. Thank You. Today, wisdom was wanted, You supplied. Thank You. You know that rest is required, and again we know that You will provide, because You are our Provider. Thank You for watching over Cathy today. Thank You for the gifts that she received from You in the form of medical treatments. You have her right where she can minister to others in a way no one else may be able to. Help her to see that she is a blessing, and a proof of Your enduring care and love in all she does and to all whom she meets. Bless her with rest and very little if any side effects from today's treatments. You are in control and we place our lives and trust in You. In Jesus name. Amen.

Thanks Tammie. So far so good.

Father, You alone know all things, and I'm certainly glad You do. You hold Cathy in the very center of Your heart, the very best place to be. Thank You for putting all the things together to take care of her in this time. You know that after the treatments she gets there is tiredness and anxiousness, and even sickness, so I ask that You draw Your hands over Your heart where Cathy is in You. Protector her, calm her, giver her rest and strength. Warm her from top to bottom with Your presence and love. In Jesus name. Amen.

Lord, I pause in the middle of this day to lift up my friend Cathy to You. You are SO very loving and gracious and I ask that Your love and grace flow down upon her in extra abundance. Whisper to het of Your love for her and only her. Remind her that she IS beautiful that she IS Your princess and nothing will EVER change that. It's fact and it's written on Your heart, so it is everlasting. Grant her rest as she is weary and the road ahead doesn't look easy or beautiful. Remind her that You are already there and when she joins You in the next moment, it will be an even more wonderful moment because the two of you will be together. In Jesus name. Amen.

Father, thank You for community of believers to journey toward deeper places with You with. Thank You for Your timing in all things. Continue to journey with Cathy and guide her in all. In Jesus name. Amen.

God thank You for instructing us to set aside a day of rest and worship. Help us to worship You in truth and love with all of our heart.
Thank You for the plans You have made for us and the lives we get to shine Your light into. Draw others we know who aren't walking with You to Yourself. Let them see the sufficiency and love and peace You bring by the working of You in our lives. In Jesus name. Amen.

Lord, this morning as our minds whirl with the what next, I ask You help us to stay in the just now moments. Help us see You in each of them and set aside our concerns about tomorrow. Be with Cathy. Relax her body and mind. Help her to focus on You. We love You, we thank You and we praise You. In Jesus name Amen.

Father, we are weary and in need of Your rest. Deep rest that can only be supplied by You. So we open our hearts, minds, and bodies to receive it. Bless Your holy name. Be with Cathy this day. Let her experience Your strength afresh and anew today. In Jesus name. Amen.

Father, bless Cathy this day with Your great and awesome love. Hold her tightly. Love on her mightily in some unique way. Thank You for the endurance You give to her each moment. Bless her and Mike today ever so deeply. In Jesus name. Amen.

I'm asking Father to at You reach out and hold Cathy's hand today. Sometimes things on this journey get a bit lonely and we need a reassuring sense of someone being with us. The best someone is You. So hold her hand in Yours and love on her. In your other hand hold onto Mike. Connecting them through You. We love You. In Jesus namr. Amen.

Father, be with my friend Cathy today. Govern her every thought, word and action. Be with Mike as he ministers to her. Guide them both into Your presence and love. Help them to relax and unwind. Give them Your joy thus day. In Jesus name. Amen.

God, Your Son promises rest to those who choose to follow Him. So I ask that Your rest overwhelm Cathy and Mike. That You replace fear with Your peace. These are available to us simply because we are Your children, so as children, we come to ask for more. More of You. Help us receive it fully and completely. In Jesus name. Amen.

Lord, the blanket of snow outside reminds me of the way you see Your children. Clean, white, pure. Thank You. Praise Your name. Be with Cathy this day. Remind her of how You are with her. Whisper to her Your great love. Thank You. Praise Your name. In Jesus name. Amen.

Lord thank You for patience and direction. Thank You for Your leading and compassion. Help us to share these things with others throughout our day. I know its extra early in the morning, but Lord, could You hear my prayer and bring deep rest to Cathy now. Give her peace and calm. Let her hear You singing over her, even now. We love You God. In Jesus name. Amen

Lord thank You for the sunshine! And wise decisions after foolish ones! You know what is best for us when we don't. And You slow us to go our own way to allow us to learn to trust You more. Thank You for not scolding or making fun of us when we realize You knew best all along. Bless Cathy and Mike as the weekend comes with lots of joy and laughter. Help them to make beautiful memories together. In Jesus name. Amen.

God, thank You for loving and caring spouses! Bless Mike today, extra specially. In Jesus name. Amen.

We worship and praise You today as the day closes, God. Bring rest and peace of mind to Cathy and Mike as they continue to trust in You. Continue to give them hope and Your joy. Thank You, Father for all You are doing and how You are moving. In Jesus name, Amen.

Lord, Cathy has a full week ahead. I know that You know this. I also know that You are already there in each and every moment of it too. Guide her. Direct her path. Help her negotiate through all of it with unyielding grace. She is Your precious princess, help her to feel that throughout each daily step. We love You Lord. In Jesus name. Amen.

Lord, medical tests take their toll on the body and mind. Give Cathy peace of mind and rest of body. Please have gentle hands preform the tests this week. Place soft and confident voices surround her. Open hearts to Your Spirit that shines through in Cathy and Mike as they interact with those around them. Bless them with Your presence. In Jesus name. Amen.

> I will have all three drugs tomorrow two chemo therapies and one immunotherapy. The pet scan showed no increase in any cancer. No spreading. I think one thing shrunk a little but basically I am stable, no decrease. She said this is a

typical response, although she would like to see a decrease of course. So the plan is to do the same three drugs this time and again in three weeks. then we will drop down to one chemotherapy drug and immunotherapy. At that point, the removal of onechemotherapy drug should reduce some of my fatigue and my need for dexamethasone which I think is cause if me more problems than the chemo. After two years, we will reevaluate and could possibly radiate any remaining cancer or keep monitoring me with pet scans. She is increasing the life expectancy because I asked about it but she is not making any predictions. She says her "goal" is more than 2 years with a smile on her face.

Sorry for too much detail, but you get the same thing as the sisters and my sons.

That is fine with me!

Did I hear something in a prayer about loving spouses that leads me to believe that things at home are going well? I pray so dear Tammie.

Yes. Things are better. I think my attitude changed...

And I am sure you were missed when you were away.

Yes!

Lord, bring rest. Deep rest. Let deep peace rest in her. Give her joy in
the middle of the rest and peace. In Jesus name. Amen.

Of course I was just lying down for a nap when I heard the buzz of this prayer. Thank you dear friend. Prayers back at you. Nancy's David could use prayer as well. I think you know of his multiple myeloma. He is having a bad week. He had been in remission and they were transitioning him to a maintenance chemo. His body didn't like the new chemo so they stopped it. I have not heard how he is since bible study in Tuesday.

Father, grant Cathy and Mike extra time with You and each other. Bless
their time with You in a wonderful manner. Show them Your grace and
give them Your peace. In Jesus name. Amen.

Brain MRI showed No new lesions. The previously radiated lesions look like scar tissue and should be dead but they will keep monitoring them every three months. In three months I will have an MRI with contrast which will show a better image. Very thankful today thanks for the prayers.

Praise God from Whom all blessings flow!
Lord You are amazing and we worship You. Continue to carry Cathy and bring Your healing to her body, mind, and spirit. In Jesus name. Amen.

> I was just looking back at your Saturday prayer when we started our Sabbath. New thing we are trying to work on. We spent more time with Jesus, our bible, our bible study, our church messages, prayer than any other weekend ever. Thank you Jesus.

Lord You are faithful and true. We thank You for Your grace and mercy. Bless Cathy and Mike today with peace and even more rest. Give them signs of You with them. In Jesus name. Amen.

God You alone reign from on high. You alone care so much for Your creation. Thank You for caring for us; for choosing us from before time began to be Your children. Guide Cathy and Mike in the decisions they make. Give them peace over each one, big or small. Help them to continue to fully rely on You for all that they are moving through. Thank You for Your blessings. In Jesus name. Amen.

God, at the close of another day blessed by Your presence, we stop to give You thanks. You are so good to us. Thank You for all You are doing and all You are going to do in Cathy and Mike's lives. Bless them this might with good rest. In Jesus name. Amen.

Lord, thank You for all the beauty of creation. It reminds us of how creative You are. And that You created us. Thank You for the relationships You give us in our lives, most especially with You. Guide us today in Your live and grace. Bless Cathy with Your beauty today. In Jesus name. Amen

> Thank you Lord Jesus.

Lord, Your blessings are so abundant. I thank You for safety and warmth. For the beauty all around. And for the eternal hope that You give. Bless Cathy this night with a warmth that starts in her very core and radiates outward. In Jesus name. Amen.

Father in the midst of chaos, You stand immovable, steady and sure. Thank You that we can anchor in You so deeply. Praise You Lord God for Your never ending love for us. Bless Cathy with the full assurance of her family members being deeply anchored in You. In Jesus name. Amen.

Lord how beautiful is the fresh snow here today?! Your love abounds in our lives and we don't deserve any of the grace You have given. All we can do is offer You praise and our hearts. So we fall at Your feet and worship You. Thank You for the movement toward You we get to make and see each day. Bless Cathy with more of Your grace today. In Jesus name. Amen.

Lord, breathe Your truth into our lives today. Truth about who You are and she we are in You. In Jesus name. Amen.

Lord as we rest in Your presence grant us more insight into Your love for us. Help us to see ourselves the way You see us and not as we see ourselves or how the world sees us. Help the beauty You have placed within shine out to those around us. Bless Cathy today with more rest and a great sense of security in You. In Jesus name. Amen.

Lord, provide for Cathy in ways that only You can. Bless her and Mike with Your holy provision. Thank You for their lives and love of You. In Jesus name. Amen.

Lord, in the cold, be the warmth for Cathy, Mike, Mark and Scott. Be their light in the dark. Draw each of them to Yourself in a magnificent way today, a way that is totally unique to each of them. Thank You for Your wonderful care of and for them. Bless them from Your throne above. In Jesus name. Amen.

Lord today we celebrate love. But Your love is perfect so I celebrate Your perfect love to me. Earthly love can be fleeting and fickle, but Your love is true, complete and everlasting. Thank You for loving me. Thank You for loving Cathy. In Jesus name. Amen.

Lord, thank You for Your care and the insight You give. Thank You for Your continued pursuit of us, even when it's uncomfortable. Bless Cathy with safety and warmth as You continue to work in her body to bring about Your glory in her life. In Jesus name. Amen.

God, You alone are true Life. We praise You for the new and eternal life that You give upon our receiving Your Son as Savior. Help us to make Jesus Lord of all parts of our being and life. Thank You for being pleased and delighted in the creation of us. Help us to continually praise and worship You. Bless Cathy with abundant living. In Jesus name. Amen.

Father, we continue to praise Your name for keeping us in Your care. You are an amazing God and we are Your beloved children. Thank You for how You have cared for Cathy. Give her the rest she needs. Please keep any side effects of the chemo to minimum. Be her and Mike's strength. In Jesus name. Amen.

Lord, continue please to having Your grace flow down upon Cathy, Mike, Mark and Scott. Be near them as the draw ever closer to You. Bring them Your joy and provision. In Jesus name. Amen.

Lord, thank You for rest, peace, and freeing us from our prisons. Thank You for the beautifulness of the sun glistening off of the snow. Thank You for keeping Cathy and Mike safe and being with them every step of their journey. Wrap them in Your warm love. In Jesus name. Amen.

> Praying for you dear Tammie.

Lord, continue to walk with Cathy. Holding her extra tightly when she needs it. Give her rest of body and mind. Help her to simply enjoy You today. In Jesus name. Amen

Lord, God, thank You for the blessing of another day. Help us to not take for granted any of the days You have for us. Help us to always remember that You are in control, not us. Bless Your holy name. We worship and praise You. Bless Cathy with a day filled with joy and peace. In Jesus name. Amen.

> Wonderful prayer for today. Thanks Tammie.
> Back at you sister.

Thank you.

Father, open our eyes to Your purposes today. Let every word and action of ours reflect You. Guide us and continue to walk beside us. In Jesus name. Amen.

Lord You are SO very wonderful! You continue to bless and we thank You for the blessing of another day. Forgive us Lord when we forget Your great daily mercies to us. We sometimes get rather wrapped up in our lives and leave You out of the every day aspects of it all. But You are always there, guiding us and willing to hear us. Thank You for staying close to Cathy and Mike and their boys. Bless them with the assurance that You haven't missed one moment of their day.
In Jesus name. Amen.

Father thank You for watching over us. Thank You for guiding us and directing us. Thank You for the life that You have given Cathy Mike and the boys. Thank you Lord for walking alongside them. I asked today that

you would guide Cathy in all things in all decisions that she would have
to make that they would be things that would glorify you. Thank You for
her life and the healing work that You're doing in her life. Jesus' name.
Amen

Lord, guide and direct Cathy today in all things. Be the peace that
passes all understanding to and for her throughout this entire day. In
Jesus name I pray. Amen.

Jesus, thank You for being the door to eternal life. The only way to that life
is through You. So simple. Thank You for Your willingness to let us in
when we come to You. Amen.

                                                                                                            Amen!

God, You are on Your throne and have chosen to give us another day to
glorify You. So, as daughters of the Most High God, we give You praise and honor.
We lift thanks to You for the very breath we breathe. Thank You Lord for Cathy and the
marvellous wonders You are doing in her life and all around her. Bless her with strength
today. Be with the family and draw them all closer to each other and You. In Jesus name.
Amen

                                        Love daughters of the Most High God!!!!

Lord, as we prepare to end our day, give us peace of mind and rest of
body. Use this night to prepare us for Your work in and around us tomorrow.
Bless Cathy with deep rest tonight, Father. Thank You for all that You ate
doing in her life. Amen.

Lord, thank You for Cathy. Thank You for the strength You have giver her
and for Your light that shines out from her. Bless her with even more of
You. Fill her to overflowing. Ease any discomfort within her. In Jesus
name. Amen.

Lord in the middle of the sunshiny day I passed the thank You for the
sunshine. And I thank you for your Son who shines within Cathy and
Mike. Help them both to know that your love is ever present and super
strong in each of them. And Jesus name I pray Amen

Thank You God for peace that passes all understanding. That can only
come from You. Thank You that Cathy knows, really knows how loved
she is by You and is super important to You. As she rests in You today,
bless her exceedingly and abundantly with the assurance that You do
have her boys secure in You. Continue to walk with Cathy and Mike.
Make their time together rich beyond measure. I ask these things in

Jesus might name. Amen.

Gracious God, watch over Cathy and Mike. Draw them super close to You. Sing over them of and with Your love. Bless them with relaxation and peace. Surround them with loving family and friends. In Jesus name. Amen.

My prayer for Cathy today Lord is that she would know the truths about her in this song: https://youtu.be/wqZ0ygLSQP8

Lord God, we praise Your name! You are good and full of mercy, grace, and truth. These are who You are. You see us and love us and I thank You for doing so. Continue to see and watch over Cathy. Give her strength, Your strength, in her times of weakness. In that weakness, shine through her completely Your love, mercy, grace, and strength. In Jesus name. Amen.

> Getting the second vaccine at 12:30. Beautiful song yesterday!

Lord protect Cathy today from any adverse reaction to the second COVID shot. Give her rest and strength afterward. Continue to be her and Mike's peace and joy. Put Your love and joy in Mark and Scott's life. In Jesus name. Amen.

Lord God Most High, thank You for another day to experience Your love! You Bring joy and peace with Your very presence. Thank You that You are doing exactly that in Cathy's heart. Help her to hold onto You. When the days seem dark, Lord, be her light. When she is tired and weary, be her rest and shelter. We love You Lord and place ourselves in Your hands. In Jesus name. Amen,

Lord God I thank You today for the bird songs that remind me that spring is just around the corner. Thank You for all that you're doing and all that you are going to do. Thank You for all the great things in Cathy's life, now and in the days to come. Bless her and Mike today with brilliant sunshine and love. Your Son is our true light, let it shine from them strongly. In Jesus name. Amen.

God Almighty, in this day I SO thank You that You go before us in all that we do. That You give us just the right words to say. You have it in Your loving care. Help us to lean into You today. Be with Cathy. Give her peace of mind, rest of body and lots of love. Bless Mike as he travels alongside her in this whole cancer journey. Draw Mark and Scott into Yourself in powerful, wonderful, and unimaginable ways. It is in Jesus name I pray. Amen.

Well, Lord, You've given us yet another day to represent You. Thank You for the opportunities that are before us today and the days that follow. Be with Cathy as she ministers to others in her life through her weaknesses. Let her be a blessing to those who encounter her. Constantly remind her that You, God, are her strength and song. In Jesus name I pray. Amen.

God you know what Cathy has that could drain her they can make her extra tired but I pray that you would give her your strength and the afterwards you would give her your rest. I pray these things in Jesus name. Amen

Lord, You know what all those chemicals are doing in Cathy's body, side effects and all. Cradle her in Your loving arms. Ease and upset insides and give her deep deep rest. Don't allow the enemy to mess with her mind or make her feel guilty about what isn't getting done. Remind her that her first and only job the rest of this week is to rest her body. In Jesus name I ask these things. Amen.

Lord thank You that You have been walking so closely with Cathy and Mike. As spring moves in, let the refreshing of life refresh them. Guide them in keeping in the moment and not worrying or fussing about what is to come. Continue to be Cathy's rest and strength. Bless her, Lord with even more of You. In Jesus name. Amen.

Lord, we are amazed at Your mighty love for us. Keep sending Cathy love notes from You. Help her to see them. Bless her with continued peace today. In Jesus name. Amen.

Lord, give Cathy rest beyond human understanding. Let Your rest go deep into her soul. Give her love notes from You all day today. In Jesus name. Amen.

                                                Thanks Tammie and back at you dear!

Lord, forgive my neglect and the wrapping up within myself these past couple of days. Help us to learn to focus better and more full on You. Continue to guide and watch over my friend Cathy. Grant her all that she needs to faithfully continue walking next to You. Hear her heart's cry and hold her to Yourself. Bless her and Mike with joy and laughter beyond measure. In Jesus name. Amen.

Father, Your love knows no bounds, and for that I rejoice! Thank You for loving us when we are unlovable. You are an amazing God!
Thank You for the little things You do that we sometimes don't notice as coming from You. Help us be more aware of Your presence each day. Continue Your work in Cathy. You are not finished with her yet, so give her Your strength and insight to continue press on, an into You. In Jesus name. Amen.

Lord, God, You alone are worthy of praise. So to You we lift our hearts and voices. You've known our end from the beginning. You O Lord are Master of all. Thank You for including us in Your plans. Lord I ask that You continue to be close to Cathy and Mike. Give them clarity and wisdom as the consider all the options before them. Give the right answers to all involved in Cathy's medical care. Most of all God, keep pouring out Your love and peace on them. In Jesus name. Amen.

God, thank You for the unchanagable-ness of You. Thank You for being near to Cathy and Mike. During the first of the week we remember Your death and resurrection, remind them that You've got this for them. You've got each next thing in Your holy hands. Let them rest in that security. In Jesus name. Amen

God is SO good!

                                                                                                           Amen!

Lord, God, another day to start another week has started for us. Thank You for giving us this blessing. Thank You for Your mercy and grace. Keep Cathy close to Your heart, close enough that if she quiets herself that she can hear it beating. Let her know that Your heart beat is the life that flows to her each and every moment. Grace her with a powerful experience of Your presence this week. You have this whole thing under control, help her to just let it go into Your hands. In Jesus name. Amen.

Father, You are our great Provider. You have provided for our every need, physical, emotional, and spiritual. You proved the way to relationship with You. You ARE amazing! Thank You that all You are providing for Cathy. For the peace that You flood her with in times of difficulty. Continue to provide what she needs. We trust You. In Jesus name. Amen.

Lord, thank You for the You keep us right next to Your heart. You have engraved our names on the very palm of Your hand. How wonderful! Lord You know the struggles Cathy faces, I ask that You give her grace beyond imagination; peace without limit; and rest the more than meets her needs. Give her wisdom and discernment that come from You. I ask these thing in Jesus name. Amen.

Father the gift from You that we remember these next days is amazing. That You would sacrifice Yourself for us! Thank You.
Guide Cathy and Mike into Your ever-loving care this day, the day we remember that You willingly made a choice to face the coming cruel death on a cross, for each of them.
Help them rest in You. In Jesus name. Amen.

Lord, that You for Your grace and incredible mercy. You are grace, mercy and love, and SO much more. Thank You for allowing us to experience You in these ways. You see us when we are hurting or full of joy. You care if we are in need of anything. You see what Cathy needs and are providing it. Sometimes we don't always see or understand what You are doing, but You are doing something. Today we remember that Friday happened to Your Son, and we know that Sunday was on its way. But Saturday seemed silent. But You were doing something. You were preparing and working and getting ready for Sunday. I know that the same happens with us. Friday is terrible, and we know Sunday is coming, but we are waiting in silence on Saturday. But You are working in the silence. So thank You for what You are doing for Cathy that we can't see. Help her to know that even in the silence You are doing something. In Jesus name. Amen.

                                                                                                                     Beautiful

God, today we celebrate the resurrection. Never before or since has someone raised themselves from the grave. But You did. And that same power lives in each who has chosen to believe. Praise Your name! thank You Lord. Be with Cathy and Mike on this day. Let them experience Your resurrection power in their hearts and lives. Make this an extra special Easter day. In Jesus name. Amen.

Father, You are our Savior. When we were at our worst, You saved us by Your blood. When we are frightened or anxious, You rescue us with Your peace. When we are sad and alone, You deliver us with Your presence. You are all things to and for us. Thank You that You care about Cathy that much and so much more. In her pain, be peace. In her confusion, be her solid rock. In her tiredness, be her rest. When she feels alone, be her refuge. We love You Lord. In Jesus name. Amen

Father, thank You for Your continued protection of Cathy. Keep her ever in Your care as she continues to journey alongside You. Love on her extra much today. In Jesus name. Amen.

Lord, bring Cathy rest today. Your rest. Ease any symptoms from current treatments as only You can do. Bring healing to her mind, body and soul. Hold her in Your loving arms gently but firmly. Let her know that You are right there with her. In Jesus name. Amen.

Lord, Your blessings are amazing, even the ones we cannot recognize. Continue to rain blessings on Cathy, Mike, Mark and Scott. Continue to give them strength that can only come from You. Bless Cathy with more rest as she recovers from this latest round of chemo. Help her body to regain what is needed to fight the foreign cells in her body. Bless her with

the sense that You are holding her in Your ever-loving arms.
In Jesus name. Amen.

Father, blanket Cathy with joy today. Surround her with warm laughter.
Wrap her in Your love and give her deep, deep rest and refreshing of
body, mind, and soul. In Jesus name. Amen.

Lord, You are the Knower of all things. You know us inside and out.
Thank You for Your love, mercy, and grace. Be with Cathy and Mike today.
Guide them into deeper relationship with You and each other. Overwhelm
with love where there is fear. Bring peace when there is chaos. Bring joy in
the middle of sadness. Give them both deep rest. In Jesus name. Amen,

Lord, today is the day we set aside to rest in and worship You more fully
than the other days of our week. We lift our praises to You because You
alone are worthy of praise. There is no other god who brings life
abundantly to it's followers. You actually desire relationship with us.
Thank You for all of that and so much more. Help Cathy today to fully rest
in Your arms as a way of worship. Let her absorb Your love and strength as she focuses on
You. As Mike ministers to her, give him a powerful sense of Your guiding him and giving him
strength. In Jesus name. Amen.

Father, thank You for my friend Cathy. Thank You for the example she is
to me and to others around her of Your grace. Your light is truly within
her. Let her never forget that. No matter where she is or who she is with,
Your light, Lord shines through. Continue to be with her, giving her strength
for each moment of the day. Help her to remember to rest, physically and
spiritually as often as she needs to. Let You arms of love hold her strongly.
In Jesus name. Amen.

Lord God, Creator of heaven and earth and all things in each, guide us in
Your love today. Help us focus on You throughout the day, leaving the
world of care behind us. Wrap Cathy in Your love. Give her and Mike all
that they need to follow Your guiding hand. In Jesus name. Amen.

Lord, You love brings joy to our hearts. Let Cathy feel both in absolute
abundance today. Give her more of Yourself. Continue to guide and walk
beside her. Work in the lives of those who are deciding on her treatment.
Let the answers that come be Your according to Your will. In Jesus
name. Amen.

Lord, pour out Your Spirit on Cathy and Mike in a new and fresh way. Let
them experience You in a way unexpected. Draw Mark and Scott to Your side.
Be their guide and strength. Let them seek You with all their hearts and minds.
Continue to bring rest and refreshing to Cathy. In Jesus name. Amen.

I was denied proton therapy on the first try. Dr is

> going to appeal. Insurance said I do not fit into their guidelines.

Ok. That bites. Lord hear our cry. Open the path for the therapy that Cathy needs. Guide those who make the decisions to Your answer. In Jesus name. Amen.

> Thanks Tammie!

You are loved. Rest in Him. He's got you.

Lord, encourage Cathy and Mike's heart today. Give them assurances of Your being in control and doing the best things for them right now, even if they don't see it or feel it or understand it. Give them the blessed gift of a super powerful sense of Your presence as they walk through this day and the days to come. Give wisdom to all those who are making decisions on treatments for Cathy. Guide them to the decisions that are Your will and Your best for her. In Jesus name. Amen.

Lord thank You for being You. We rejoice in all that You are. Because You are love You love us. Because You are peace You bring peace to our lives. Thank You for Cathy. Continue to love on her. Continue to be her peace. Bring rest and refreshment to her heart, body, mind, and soul. I ask these things in Jesus name. Amen.

Lord, continue to walk with Cathy in this difficult time. Hold her close today and be her strength for everything she will face. Be the very breath in her lungs, and every thought in her mind. She is Your child. Your princess. Let her know that she is not alone, ever. You are right there with her, so hold her close today and all the days to come. In the mighty name of Jesus, Amen.

> Love the very breath in her lungs!

He is you know!

> Yes. I know. Need reminders. Thank you.

Good morning God. Thank You for the rest You give us, physical, emotional, and spiritual. Be with Cathy. Fill her from the inside out with You today and all the today's to come. Bless her and Mike with time together this week. In Jesus name. Amen.

How wonderful are Your works God. We rejoice and give thanks to You for all of them. God, here in Indiana, as I look out my window, I'm amazed at You creativity. Snow blankets the ground, in April! How beautiful! Bring Cathy gentle and wonderful surprises of Yourself and Your love for her. Things to extol Your majesty. Things that bring comfort and joy. In Jesus name. Amen.

Lord God place Your hand on Cathy, let it be there for all day and all days to come. She is Your daughter, royalty. Continue to extend Your grace to Your beloved daughter. Let her know that she is fully loved. In Jesus name. Amen.

Lord, guide Cathy and Mike today in all the decisions that they are faced with. Give them Your peace about the direction that they choose. Hold them in Your loving arms. Be their rest and joy. In Jesus name. Amen.

Lord, keep Cathy close to Your heart. Give her assurance that You are forever caring for and loving her. Warm her with Your love. Guide her and hold her in Your peace. In Jesus name. Amen

Father today we worship You, or rather focus more on worshiping You. You are almighty, ever-loving, and eternal. You have planted eternity in our hearts. We thank You for that. We await Your timing and You will in all things that are moving in our lives.. Bless Cathy today with patience as she awaits the next thing You are preparing for her. You are already there waiting with open arms and hearts. We love You. In Jesus name. Amen.

Lord, thank you for the sunshine and how Your Son shines in our lives. Shine brightly today in her and throughout these coming days. Bless her with more and more of You. In Jesus name. Amen.

Lord, be King in our lives. As we bow before You in worship and prayer, let us be reminded that You alone are Ruler over us. Help us submit to Your will, no matter how difficult it may be.
Bless Cathy as she abides deeply in You with Your great peace and love. In Jesus name. Amen

Lord, You are great. Your presence is such a blessing. Help us to not take it for granted. You are gracious and merciful. Thank You for extending Your grace and mercy to us. Blanket Cathy with Your mighty love. In Jesus name. Amen.

God, thank You that You continue to walk with Cathy and Mike. Bring them an overwhelming, joyous sense of Your peace today! Let Your love surround them in the difficulties they face. In Jesus name. Amen.

God, thank You for Your marvelous works. Thank You for the things that You are working in us and through us. Thank You for burdens lifted. We praise You, Father for who You are. Bless Cathy and Mike with even more peace than they thought was possible. Draw Mark and Scott to Your side. Bring healing and rest to all of these blessed family. Fill each of their homes with Your peace and Spirit. In the wonderful name of Jesus I pray. Amen

Lord, we began a new month here. One that promises warmth and flower and fully leaved trees. Thank You for that. More than that thank You for Your promises to never leave us and to live within us. So God, when we are particularly lonely or alone, remind us that we really aren't. There is no place we can go that You won't be. Praise You for that and so much more. In Jesus name. Amen.

Father, bless Cathy today with the fullness and richness on Your Word. Reveal Your promises to her. Let her rest totally in You. In Jesus name. Amen.

God, Your blessings are new every morning. You are our treasure and great reward. Thank You for the gift of a new day with You. Your healing touch is needed, so please Lord, reach down and touch where there is pain. Touch where there is cancer. Touch were there is weariness. Touch where there is doubt. Bless Cathy with Your special touch and comfort today. In Jesus name, Amen.

Lord, thank You for Your care of us. And thank You for the rain too. As the thunder roars it reminds me of Your power and majesty.
You have blessed us with Your gentle care. Continue to bless Cathy with Your gentleness and love. In Jesus name. Amen.

How marvelous are Your works O Lord. How vast the sum of them! I lift my praises to You, God of the universe. For Your blessings upon us are so undeserved. Your mercies are unbelievable. Thank you for clearing images and new treatments. Bless Cathy with rest and pain relief.
In Jesus name. Amen

God please bless Cathy with overflowing rest this day. Rest of body, mind, and soul. Let her feel totally secure in Your loving arms. In Jesus name. Amen.

> Right when I was having a bad day yesterday, your text came through!
>
> Thank you dear friend!

God knows what's needed and when.

Lord, You alone know what lies ahead. We place our trust in You. Help us to keep our hearts and minds focused on You. Whisper gently into Cathy of Your total love for her. You delight in her every moment of the day, Lord. You lavish love and grace and mercy every minute. Help her to really sense it, especially during the difficult. Thank You Father for all You are accomplishing in her and through her. In Jesus name. Amen.

Lord, thank You that You never leave us alone. You are always with us, even when we can't feel You. Wrap Cathy in Your loving presence. Ease the side effects of her treatments. Gently help her see You today. Let her know that rest is just another way she can worship You.
In Jesus name. Amen.

God, all I ask for, for Cathy tonight is rest beyond imagination. In the powerful name of Jesus. Amen!

Father, thank You for a fresh new day. A day of hope and You. Keep us ever in Your holy hands. It is in You alone we trust with our very lives. There is no better place for us to be. Remind Cathy of Your love and care. Help her to endure these treatments and their side effects. Help her be gentle to herself while You are caring, lovingly for her. In Jesus name. Amen

God, You ARE our strength and refuge. Let us hide in You today. Be our strength in the hard things today.
Bring rest and healing to Cathy in a super way today and all her tomorrows. In Jesus name, Amen.

Lord, God, Holy one, we worship You in the midst of pain and chaos. You alone have the power to bring healing, whether through medical means or divine intervention. We trust Your path to this. We place our lives in Your hands. Bless Cathy with the rest and healing that she needs. Help her nourish her body, mind, and soul today. In Jesus name. Amen.

WordGo BSF Bible Study App. Personal or Group Study Options Available. Didn't know if you know about this resource.

Lord, thank You for renewing us each day. Thank You for all the possibilities You have set before us in this new day. Help us to be aware of where You are in each moment. Bless Cathy today with the joy of Your presence no matter what she is going through. In Jesus name. Amen.

Lord, all creation rejoices. Let us join them in lifting praise to You. Thank You for the small, even seemingly tiny, victories. Thank You for Your care of Cathy and the family. Continue to be their peace that passes all understanding. In Jesus name. Amen.
FYI: The word amen means: let it be so.

Lord God, Father and Friend, we lift up our praises to you. No matter how dark it seems You are Light. No matter how lost and alone we feel, You are Hope. No matter what is happening all around us, You are Peace and Calm. You simply Are, The I Am. The never changing, all

powerful, Creator of the universe and so much more. Thank You for
seeing us and loving us. Watch over Cathy in Your gentleness and be to
her everything she needs today. In Jesus name. Amen.

Father, great is Your name and greatly to be praised. We praise You
Father for all that You are and will be in our life. Bless Cathy today with
patience in the process. With hope in You and what You are up to.
And with rest in Your arms. In Jesus name. Amen.

> Thank you dear Tammie. My patience is running low at times. Thanks for the specific prayer. Back at you dear friend.

Thank you.

Father, You are wonderful! You meet us where we are and love us no
matter how messy we are. Thank You for loving us so richly and deeply.
In Your rich love, lavish it down on Cathy today. Be the strength that she
needs to get to each next moment. Nourish her body and soul with good
things from You. And, Father, when it gets to be too much, hold her as
she cries. Let her know that You are in fact carrying her. In Jesus name.
Amen.

> Beautiful prayer today. Today is chemo and proton therapy and 3 doctor appointments. Pretty amazing. I pray I am doing something with this life that pleases God.

You are!
Sister, what a song!
Perfect for you!

https://m.youtube.com/watch?v=l6sX4Vw8mx0 **The God Who Sees**

Father, today I was reminded that Your mercies our new every morning.
We don't borrow from tomorrow and we don't have to use leftovers from
yesterday. We get a new batch every day. Thank You for that give Cathy
all the mercies, blessings, and Grace that she needs to get through this day.
Bless Mike with the ability to be weak sometimes, so that Your strength
shines through him. In Jesus name. Amen.

Lord, today, in Your great mercy and grace, cover Cathy with Your mercy,
grace and wonderful love too. Be with her in a strong way as she walks
this difficult healing path. Let all the parts of this process work in her
body to do exactly what it is meant to do. Guide her gently, Lord God,
in all she says and does. In Jesus name. Amen.

Lord, we do trust You in all things. Yet sometimes the all things are a bit
difficult to do that in. So I ask that when our trust weak, You grant us
more faith so that we can trust You more. In our weakness, show Yourself

strong though us. Watch over Cathy today with Your tender mercies.
In Jesus name. Amen.

God thank You for giving us another day to serve You and be served by
You. Your grace is SO wonderful, and Your mercies never end. Thank You.
Be with Cathy and Mike today. Bring them joy in being with one another
and You. Extend Your living arms around each of them and their boys.
Guide them all in Your peace and test. In Jesus name, I pray. Amen.

Lord, You have granted us another day where we can bring praise and
worship to You. Sometimes our offerings if praise and worship seem so
small and insignificant, but they are not that way to You. One moment
spent in Your presence is greater than millions of moments anywhere else.
So in this moment, let is praise You and be with You. And the next moments
to come as well. Bring super rest to Cathy today, as she spends moments with
You and her family. In Jesus name. Amen

Thank You Father for the breath in our lungs and the thoughts of our
minds. Each of which We can turn to You in worship, prayer, and praise.
Be the very breath in Cathy's lungs today and occupy her mind with
thoughts of You. In Jesus name. Amen.

> Tammie dear, I pray over these individually but as a group
> they are fabulous too! Thank you so very much. Prayers for
> you my friend as well!

Father, You are above all and in control of all. You know our next step
and each of our tomorrows. You bless us each day beyond anything that
we deserve. Thank You for loving us. Be with Cathy today. Extend to her
Your strength and grace. Give her rest and bring healing to her body. Keep her in Your
tender care. In Jesus name. Amen.

God, we love You and we worship You alone. You are our only hope.
Help us hold onto You in each storm and stay close to You in every calm.
Continue to encounter Cathy in every moment. Hold her hand as You
hold her heart. In Jesus name. Amen.

Lord, as You direct our day, help us to see You in each step we take with
You. Continue to guide Cathy and the medical staff providing her care. Give
rest to her and Mike as they keep up with all the appointments and care
that is required. You are in complete control. Help us all to rest in You. In
Jesus name. Amen.

Lord, the overnight rain reminds me of the refreshing that You bring
during my life. Sometimes in the dark too. Bless Cathy with the refreshing
rain of You. In Jesus name. Amen.

Lord, You are ever SO faithful. You have given us another day to rejoice in You. Life here isn't always easy or wonderful, You know that, You've been here and done that. But God You are steadfast and sure, never changing. So we praise You. Thank You for all You are doing in and around Cathy. Bless her today with Your tenderness. Show her something special today that points to You. In Jesus name. Amen.

Father, shower Cathy with Your amazing grace. Let her hear it ringing in the depths of her soul the song You sing over her in delight of her. You are all wise and wonderful and we place our lives in Your hands. In Jesus name. Amen.

Father, we are ever grateful for Your presence and love that walks with us each moment of the day. Help us to seek Your presence and accept Your love each moment. Continue Your walk with Cathy. Continue to be with her every moment. Bless her with even more of You. In Jesus name. Amen.

Father, rain down joy and laughter for Cathy and Mike. Help them to laugh at something today, big or small. Be with them in Your joy. In Jesus name. Amen.

Father, You have given us another new day. Here the rain is washing everything clean. There is the brilliant aroma of the rain all around. Thank You for washing us clean and making us an aroma of you. Be with Cathy today. Be her refreshing and as she shines for You bless her with the brilliant aroma of Yourself. In Jesus name. Amen

Lord as this day begins to close, wrap Cathy in Your powerful and wonderful arms. Guide her gently to sleep tonight. Give her deep deep rest. In Jesus name. Amen.

Lord, thank you for the presence of Your Holy Spirit and the life He brings to mind. You know long before we do what it is that we need. You prepare to meet those needs even before we ask. Thank You for taking such good care of Cathy. Thank You for asking beside her and holding her close. Be with her today in everything that she has to face. Remind her that You truly do have everything taken care of for her and are right there with her. In Jesus name. Amen.

        Praying the same for you dear friend. I am at proton therapy, then have a CT. I drove myself to DC and we have severe thunderstorms. Should be lots of traffic when I leave here about 2:30. Hope you are well. Any specific prayer requests? How are you?

I'm doing ok. I sprained some ligaments in my replaced knee. Hot air balloon ride had a rather rough landing. It is taking a long time to heal.

> OMG. You made me giggle with the hot are balloon ride! Sorry about the ligaments. I hear they take longer to heal than bones sometimes.
>
> When are you jumping from a plane?

They do. The ride part was fun but the landing not so much.
I draw the line at the jumping out if perfectly good flying planes! I do have some sense. HA!

> Hahaha. Yes you do!

You drove yourself? To DC? You're crazier than me then.

Lord, thank You for the strength You have given Cathy to have some control over her treatments. Continue to guide her and her medical team on this path. Bless Cathy with exceeding rest and peace today. Help her and Mike to see You in this very day as they rest and trust in You. In Jesus name. Amen.

Father, You are above all. You are majestic and wonderful. You are holy and gracious. Thank You for the blessing of being Your child and the way You care for each of Your children. Be close to Cathy today as she worships and gives You praise. Bring continued rest and peace to her life. In Jesus name. Amen.

> It's a good day. Thank you Jesus. I am doing better than expected with proton therapy side effects. Except the rash. Kinda like poison ivy.

What a blessing! God is SO good!

> So good. How are you my dear?

Healing well. Muscles are made at me, but the ligaments seem to be nearly healed. Gotta work at being own PT and get the muscles back in line with life.

Lord God, as Your blessings flow into our lives, we offer to You our praise and adoration. It is with grateful hearts that we enter this day with You. Thank You for the rest our bodies and minds received overnight. Continue to care for Cathy in Your wonderful, gentle way. Guide her in the decisions that she makes. Bless her with Your peace as she continues her treatments. In Jesus name. Amen.

Jesus, we adore You. You are above and beyond anything we can think. You are amazing. Nothing escapes Your notice. Nothing thwarts Your plans. And You love us! Thank You. Be with Cathy and Mike. Bring them joy as they continue to make marvelous memories together. In Jesus name. Amen.

Enter his gates with thanksgiving, and his courts with praise! Give thanks to him; bless his name! For the Lord is good; his steadfast love endures forever, and his faithfulness to all generations.
Psalm 100:4-5 ESV

Lord thank You for Your Word. It speaks nothing but Truth to us. And You Lord, are Truth. Continue to strengthen Cathy with Your Truth, with Yourself. Bless her heart and mind with Your Word. Bless her body with Your rest and healing. In Jesus name. Amen.

Lord, continue to bring Yourself to Cathy. Be all that she needs today. Hold her fast to Your heart. Overwhelm her with peace. In Jesus name. Amen.

Lord God, thank You for being so kind and gentle. For holding us like a child to her mother's breast. For nourishing our inner being with Your love and mercy. As You walk today with Cathy, show her how You delight in her and are proud of her. Continue to give her strength in this battle. We love You and pray these things in Jesus name. Amen.

Father, You move every so gently in our lives, drawing us to Yourself. Thank You for You gentle patience with us.
Thank You for the grace You have extended to Cathy. Help her fill her lungs not just with the air about her, but with Your Spirit as well. Guide her every step and surround her with Your wonderful grace. In Jesus name. Amen.

> This came in during my walk while I was trying to increase my lung capacity. "Puff up my lungs" as my doctor says. I usually walk and pray so this is a great analogy! Today Mike was with me so we walked and talked.
>
> Thank you friend!!

Lord our day is closing here. I ask for rest of weary bodies and minds. Collect us into Your arms and bring us deep refreshing sleep. In Jesus name. Amen

Father, thank You for Your care for Cathy. You are wonderful an we praise You for all that you are enabling Cathy to do right now. You are working deeply inside of her and doing things that we can't even imagine. Continue to be her peace and rest, and the very breath she breathes. In Jesus name. Amen.

Thank You Lord for Your gentle breeze, Your Holy Spirit, that moves in our lives. Thank You for the peace You bring as the Holy Spirit moves in us. You alone God, know the outcome of this day for us. And we know that You are with us each step in it. So we rejoice in each moment that we walk with You. Bless Cathy with many many close moments with You today. In Jesus name. Amen.

> My proton therapy tech sang how great thou art with me!

Lord night is falling, but You are here in Your wonderful light. You bring light wherever You are. You shine brightly in Cathy in all that she does. Thank You for Your presence in and with her. Guide her into a super night's rest. Let Your light continue to shine in and through her. In Jesus name. Amen.

> Omg. My nurse for the 35 treatments told me today that I was a light...more to that by you get the connection. Much love and praying this back to you my dear.

Father, thank You for another day to celebrate Your grace and mercy. Help us to see the way You are working in our lives and through us. Bless Cathy with continued resilience in all that she does. Help to be still with You and hear Your voice. Bless her with a great sense of Your presence in her today. In Jesus name. Amen.

> You too Tammie!

I'm heading to Ohio tomorrow for a week seminar. One of my final ones in my Formational Prayer/ Healing Care program. In August I go to OH to do my first residency for the Spiritual Director studies I've started, so I can become a Spiritual Director. God is opening so many doors for me to minister His love through. I'm more than blessed.

Father, we welcome a new day with joy and open hearts. May we open ourselves to a new vision of who You are and who we are in You. Bless Cathy with new insights into how You are moving in her life and the lives of the ones she loves. Thank You for her. In Jesus name. Amen.

Father, we lift our voices to You in worship and praise, remembering that Your Spirit is the very breath that we breathe. You amazingly give us all that we need, but the overflow us with SO much more. Thank You for Your lavish grace and mercy. Please continue to walk closely with Cathy and Mike as they look to You for their strength and rely on You for each next moment. In Jesus name. Amen.

> Praying for a rich time in learning, growth and love of Jesus during your time in Ohio. Wow Tammie, so many opportunities to share Jesus to add to the ones you already have. You are really blooming where you are planted. You will do great! Wow, Spiritual Director.

God is doing some really cool stuff and has invited me along.
I am so excited to be a part of what He is doing!

Father, they way You created us is amazing. Thank You for the intricate ways each part works with each part. Thank You for the healing you are bringing from the treatments to Cathy. Give her rest. In Jesus name. Amen.

Hope you had a good day Miss Tammie!

I did!

May God bless you, Ms. Cathy with rest, joy, peace, and continued healing. In Jesus name. Amen.

Lord as Cathy walks this morning, be her every step and her every breath. Be with the conversation. May she and who she walks with be encouraged by each other and You. Bless them and keep them safe. In Jesus name, I pray. Amen.

Father, watch over Cathy and Mike as they rest their physical bodies. Refresh their souls with Your rest this night. Be their all in all. In Jesus name. Amen

And Tammie!

Father, thank You for bringing nourishment to our souls and to our bodies. Help us to wisely choose what to put into each as we go through our days. Let them be things that help us grow in You.
Thank You for Cathy and all You are working in her life. Continue to walk alongside or carry her as she has need. In Jesus name. Amen.

Lord thank You for placing people of healing in our lives. For their pouring into our lives. For the healings they carry to us from You. Continue to bring to Cathy people to pour into her as You continue to bring her healing. In Jesus name, Amen.

Father, that You for being our Father. Thank You for welcoming us as Your children, and into Your eternal kingdom. There is nothing we did or can do to deserve it. You just said "Come." Thank You for how You are going to meet us in this day. Shine brightly on Cathy today as she worships You. In Jesus name. Amen.

Praise the name if our great God. I will say it again praise the name of God. He inhabits the praise of His people. So Lord as we praise You, fill us with Yourself. Be with Cathy as she rests and praises You. Bring her peace and joy as she looks to You, her hope. In Jesus name. Amen.

Lord thank You for Your rest that sustains us through each moment of every day. Without it we would be lost. Whisper gently to Cathy of You love and delight in her, just as she is. Remind her that she is welcome into Your love just as she comes. There is nothing that she can do to earn a place in You. She has one that she cannot lose. In Jesus name. Amen.

Father thank You for calling us to Yourself. We would be so lost without Your direction. Thank You for being so close to Cathy and Mike. For walking with them so faithfully. Continue to bring healing to Cathy's body. Give her rest that exceeds anything she has ever known. Give her continued strength to walk with You. In Jesus name. Amen.

Lord God, thank You for how You lead us each day to Your heart as we open ourselves to You. Continue to draw Cathy, Mike, and their family to Yourself. Bring each of them a unique sense of You today that cannot be denied. In Jesus name. Amen.

God, we lift up our eyes to You from whom our help comes from. We find intimate refuge and abiding peace in You alone. Thank You for being here for us each and every day. Guide Cathy today into that refuge and peace that is You and help her to abide there. In Jesus name. Amen

Father thank You for joining us together in Your love. Be with Cathy today and let her enjoy Your love today in a great way. In Jesus name. Amen.

> Praying for you my friend too!

Lord, thank You for Your grace. We couldn't live without it. Help us to extend that grace to others in our lives today. In Jesus name. Amen.

Father, thank You for Your wisdom and knowledge. Thank You that, as we tune into Your heart and mind, we can experience them in our own lives. Continue to wisely guide Cathy and Mike, in Your wisdom and give them the knowledge that they need straight from Your heart. Give them peace and added rest. In Jesus name. Amen.

Lord, Your peace is invaluable, yet You give it freely. Extend Your peace to Cathy in a powerful way. Let her experience Your presence today as she never has before. Let her rest in the fact that You are in TOTAL control. Seal her from any attacks of the enemy.
In Jesus name. Amen.

Father continue to shine Your live and light into and through Cathy. Thank You that You walk right with her step by step. In Jesus name. Amen.

Lord, Your ways are wonderful, we know that full well. Sometimes we don't understand them, but we trust You in the middle of our not understanding. You and Your ways are perfect and we place our trust in You. Guide and direct all the healing that is happening in Cathy's body, mind, and soul. As she breathes, strengthen her lungs. Help her body absorb the nutrients she needs. I thank You Lord God for all that You have done and are doing in her life. In Jesus name. Amen.

Father, Your Word is wonderful. It speaks Truth into every area of our lives. Help us to continually be in Your Word so that we can know Your heart better. So that we can know You better. And so we can know ourselves better. Continue to strengthen Cathy with Yourself. Bring her both peace and joy today as she seeks You. In Jesus name. Amen.

> Amen. Beautiful Tammie!

Father, for a good rest we offer our thanks to You. For the blessing of another day, we rejoice. Give Cathy the very things she needs physically, emotionally, and spiritually, to move her through this day to a closer place beside You. Be the very breath she breathes and the very thoughts she thinks. Help he keep her mind on the things that are worthy and eternal and let the earthly and temporal pass through without leaving an imprint. Today let her focus be on the very moment she is in. In Jesus name. Amen.

Father, joy is from You, and it is in that joy that we worship You today. Joyfully we thank You and praise You for seeing us through another night of rest. In Joy we place our hearts before You and ask for another dose of Your merry, grace, and love. And in joy we receive it unto ourselves. Keep Cathy at the very epicenter of Your joy. In Jesus name. Amen.

Lord, Your grace is sufficient for all that You allow into our lives. Help us accept and make use of that grace in a bold manner. Be with Cathy today in a bold way. Let her feel Your rest and grace. In Jesus name. Amen.

Father, whatever Cathy has to do today, let her know of You presence right there with her. Let her know she is Your special daughter. That nothing cal ever change that. Bless her with a deep sense of Your Holy Presence today. In Jesus name. Amen.

Father in heaven, as this day begins, shower blessing of goodness, joy, peace, and healing of all kinds upon Cathy. Let her be the carrier of Your presence in a mighty way this day and the many days that follow. Guide the continuing medical care to exactly where You want it to be. We live You Lord and praise Your name at all times. In Jesus name. Amen.

Lord, thank You for being ever-present with us. Thank You that no matter what You are always right with us. Nothing that happens are You unaware of. Thank You for loving us. Be with Cathy today. Bring her Your peace and wonderment of the world around her. Help her to relax in You. In Jesus name. Amen.

Lord, than You for guiding and being with Cathy. Bring her extra energy today and this weekend. Give her good solid rest of body, mind and soul. We rejoice in all You do. In Jesus name. Amen.

Father, thank You for the safety and security You bring to our lives. Bless Cathy and Mike with a strong presence of both from You today. In Jesus name. Amen.

God, we worship You in Your completeness today as Father, Son, and Spirit. One does not exist without the other and we don't exist and fully live without You. You complete us. Thank You for allowing us to offer our meager sacrifices of worship to You. You accept it with joy, and it is with joy today we give it. Bring Cathy a great experience if worship today. In Jesus name. Amen.

> Oh thank you Tammie. I have had a great experience of worship today and I pray you have too!

I did!

Father thank You for the life You give us. The eternal life that we can live in right now and the forever to come. Guide all that Cathy does today. Let nothing come her way that hasn't gone through Your mighty hands. Thank You for her life and friendship. In Jesus name. Amen.

God, thank You for Your tender care and watchfulness over us. Thank You for working in us even if we don't see anything happening. Continue to heal Cathy in all ways, body, mind, soul, and spirit. Draw her to Yourself. Calm any fears with Your peace. Direct her feet on the paths You have set for her. In Jesus name. Amen.

> I am praying your prayer back at you still. I know I told you that before. Just a reminder.

I appreciate it. Very much.

Lord, be the air in Cathy's lungs. Coat them with protection from the harsh side effects. In Jesus name. Amen.

Father, as Cathy recovers from this latest round of chemo, be her Healing. Help her lungs to heal. Be each gentle breath that she takes. Bring strength back into her body. Be her Rest as she rests. Hold her tight to Yourself. In Jesus name. Amen.

> Beautiful Tammie. Makes me feel better! Truly. I will hold your prayer close in the coming days!

And I will keep praying.

> Thank you Tammie. I am doing better than last time on days one and two. Thank you Jesus!!

That's WONDERFUL! God is so good!

Lord, gently God Cathy in Your loving arms as she recovers from this latest round of chemo. Give her the needed rest for her body. Help her to get the nourishment she needs. Be the very breath in her lungs. Fill her mind with images of You. In Jesus name. Amen.

Father, we reach out to You in our lives to worship You. Thank You for Your presence in our lives. Thank You for the healing You are accomplishing in Cathy's life. Continue Your gentle way with her. Give her the needed rest. Continue to nourish her. Continue lie lavishly love on her and sing over her. In Jesus name. Amen.

Thank You Father God for another day set aside to focus on You. Let us see You for who You are and not who we want You to be. You are love and mercy and grace. You are gentle and kind and holy. You love and us grant us all things in Christ, our brother. We praise You for what You are doing in Cathy's life. You are the one in control. Be with her as she continues to heal and recover her strength so that she can worship You all the more. In Jesus name. Amen.

God, thank You for blessing us with Your Holy Spirit and having Him live in us. Lord I ask that You make us more aware of His presence today and the days that follow. That we would know each moment His power within. Thank You for that power to live as Jesus did. Without Him we would be lost. Be with Cathy today as she continues to heal. Be her strength and power to so the things You have set for her to do. Help her find stillness within so she can hear from You in a wonderful way today. In Jesus name. Amen.

> Prayed for my friend, Tammie too!

Father, Your presence in our lives is the key to living itself. Thank You for that. Thank You that when we question things the answer mist valuable that You bring is Yourself. In the tough questions, help us let that be more than enough. Help us to sit with You and require nothing else. Thank You that You are with Cathy and You are The Answer to everything for her. Bless her with peace and rest today. In Jesus name. Amen.

Father, thank You for Your rest. Bless Your Name as the only true God. We worship You and You alone. Guide us in this day to do all things as a representative of You. Let others see in us Your grace and mercy and want it for themselves. Bless Cathy today with Your grace. Guide her path and be with her every step. In Jesus name. Amen.

Lord Jesus, we praise Your name. We worship You and You alone. You are our guide. Our comfort. Our Great Shepherd. You keep us well cared for and we offer up to You our praises. Bless Cathy with Your tender care. Bring her renewed strength. Breathe into her Your love. Thank You Lord. In Jesus name. Amen.

Father, You feed our soul and provide for us all things. Thank You. Bring nourishment to Cathy, body, mind, soul, and spirit. Refresh her. Strengthen her on this journey. Be all that she needs. In Jesus name. Amen.

Father thank You so much for Your rest and peace. We so need both. Thank You for Your full provision to us each day. Be with Cathy and Mike this weekend and be their continued hope, joy, rest, and peace. In Jesus name. Amen.

God, we praise and worship You. We now at Your feet in humble adoration. You lift us up and we exalt Your Holy name this day. Thank You for watching over Cathy. For being her all in all. Continue to strengthen her body. Continue to give her rest and peace. As she experiences each moment of this day, help her to see You. In any discouragement, Father, bring her Your powerful presence. Let her know that she is not alone. Thank You. In Jesus name. Amen.

> I wanted to let you know that the pet scan and MRI were basically stable. I am very thankful!

Lord, we praise You! Thank You for this stability in Cathy's scans! You alone are our stable rock and security. You have just proved it again in Cathy. Continue to bring her to health and healing. Continue to hold her as she holds fast to You. Bless her with a rejoicing spirit today and always. In Jesus name. Amen.

Father a new day has arisen for us. Thank You for the rest overnight You provided. Praise You God for the work You are doing in Cathy's body. You have a plan and purpose for her and You are walking it out with her. Continue to strengthen her. In Jesus name. Amen.

Lord thank You for Your patience with us. For proving over and over that

You have things under Your control and perfect timing.
Continue to bring peace and healing to Cathy. In the waiting draw nearer to her, Mike, and the rest of her family. In Jesus name. Amen

Lord, thank You for all that You are. We love what You do for us and with us. But the reason we praise You is because You alone are God. For no other reason You are worthy of honor, glory, and praise. So we lift our hands and hearts to You in praise and adoration. We bow our heads, hearts, and knees in awe and reverence. Bless Cathy with more rest, peace, and Your life giving presence. In Jesus name. Amen.

Lord, thank you for the marvelously, wonderful way You take care of us. For protecting and sustaining us each day. Thank You for the challenges You walk with us through. Continue to walk with Cathy and Mike in the challenges they face. Continue to heal and refresh and renew. In Jesus name. Amen.

Father be with Cathy and Mike today. Be their continued strength. Bring Your presence in a special way. Thank You for all you are doing. In Jesus name. Amen.

Lord bless Cathy with a spirit of worship this day. Bring her joy and dancing. In Jesus name. Amen.

My friend, I am in Ashland Ohio doing my first residency for becoming a Spiritual Director. One and a half days done. Exhausted doesn't quite match how I feel right now. But OH how wonderful this is to be learning this stuff! Please pray about my knee. Its still not well. The pain and swelling is bad today.

Praying. Glad to have this specific request. I have been praying about the Spiritual Director position. Glad you are receiving this wonderful training. Praying for a refreshing nights sleep.

Thank you for reaching out. I am delighted to pray for you

I love you! Thanks!

I love you to miss Tammie. Sleep well my friend.

Lord, bless my friend Cathy, with never ending joy in her heart. Let laughter rise up within her. Let her feel free to dance to the music inside her. Be right beside her in all that she is navigating. Keep her safe. Thank You that you love us so much and we can worship You. In Jesus name. Amen.

Lord God of heaven and earth, thank You for Your love for us and for revealing Yourself to us in such beautiful ways. Bless Cathy with beauty today. In Jesus name. Amen.

> I just left my neighbors butterfly garden. Hope the knee is better

Thank you.

Lord continue to shine brightly in Cathy's life. Bless her with a tremendous amount of grace today. In Jesus name. Amen.

Lord, thank you for needed rest. Bless Cathy with rest today. And your overwhelming peace. In Jesus name. Amen

Father, blessed be Your name in all the earth. Let Your children rejoice always in You. Thank You for keeping us in Your tender care. Thank You for the wisdom You provide to help us through each thing that comes into our path of life. Help us to not forget that you have our lives totally in Your hands. Bless Cathy today with a beautiful sense of home, because wherever she is You are, and that is Home. In Jesus name. Amen.

> Let me know when that knee is better

I have a doctor's appointment on Monday afternoon. I'm hoping to get some answers to the issues with it. And maybe have the swelling drained...not looking forward to that part, by I think it is really needed.

> Glad you are going to the doctor. If the knee is drained, it should feel much better. Let me know how it goes. I am praying. How did the spiritual director training go? Or do I even need to ask. I am sure it was awesome!!!!

It was GREAT! We learned things and got to actually practice the skills on a partner. My brain is on super load. This combined with the prayer counseling and healing care I do is going to be amazing!

> So wonderful! Grateful or your experience!

Lord, we worship and praise You! You alone are worthy. We humble ourselves before You. Thank You God for all your movement in our lives. Bless Cathy with strength and grace today. In Jesus name. Amen.

Gracious Father, thank You for the sun that comes up every day to warm the earth. Thank You for the seasons Your have created to give us different kinds of beauty to enjoy. Thank You that you are at work in Cathy's life and body. Bless her with continued healing and strength. Continue to shine in her so that the people she comes in contact with her see you shining through in an effortless way. In Jesus name. Amen.

Saw knee Dr. He took a sample of fluid to test for infection, which we are both rather sure it's not. I have to have a bone scan done so he can see if I my have fractured my tibia near the implant. It is complicated to describe, but is a possibility. He also indicated that the swelling and discoloration may take some months yet to go away from the major bruise I incurred inside the knee. So now I wait for the scan place to get me in and then for Dr to read said scan to see how we move forward.

> I understand. I will be praying. Does it keep you from walking?

Thank you. Nope. Have cane, will travel.

> Well, good. We can't have Tammie immobile. You have places to go

Lord, thank You for Your presence in time of need. Thank You that you can be everywhere with all of your children at once. Bless Cathy today with your presence and guidance. In Jesus name. Amen

I have been scheduled for a nuclear bone scan for next Thursday (8/26). I go in at 7:45 am for about 30 minutes (they radio-activate me), then go back at 11 am for the scan itself.

> Well, you are in good radioactive company with me. This test should really tell them what is happening and get you on the road to recovery.

I pray so.

Lord, as we close our day, we find refuge in You. You care our security. We rely on no other. Keep Cathy in Your loving arms and give her deep rest tonight. In Jesus name. Amen.

Father thank You for watching over us. For guiding us and directing us each day. We couldn't do it without You. Continue to guide and direct Cathy and Mike closer to You each day. I thank You for what you are doing in their lives. In Jesus name. Amen.

God, You are too marvelous for words. You love us in spite of ourselves.
Thank You is all I can offer in response. Bless Cathy today with your overwhelming love. Let her bask in it. Remind her, through your creation, that she is dearly loved. In Jesus name. Amen.

Father this day is coming to an end. You have been in every moment of it in some way. Thank You for Your faithfulness to us. Bless Cathy and Mike with Your rest and tender care tonight. Bless them as the rest in Your care. Prepare them even now for Your Sabbath. In Jesus name. Amen.

Lord God, You are Lord over all and we are grateful to be called Your children. As we worship You on this day that we have set aside, may what you hear from us be beautiful to Your eats. May our worship shine in the darkness as a beacon for others to draw near to. Thank You for things that you are doing there in Maryland with Cathy and Mike. Bless them and their boys as they go about living for You. In Jesus name. Amen.

Father, thank you for the blessings of the day. The simple things we take for granted like, sunshine and rain, we thank You for. Help us to not forget that you are in the simple, everyday, moments of our lives. Help us to be ever grateful of each one of them. Bless Cathy with a great night's rest in your arms. In Jesus name. Amen.

God, thank you for life. Your life abundant and freely flowing within us. Help Cathy hold onto the hope that this kind of abundant life is hers right now where she us at. That Your Spirit flows freely in and through her. You are her rock. In Jesus name. Amen.

Father, thank You for continuously caring for us. You watch over us day and night. You are with us each moment of our time here. Thank You. Be with Cathy today. Assure her in times of discouragement that you understand and care truly walking with her. Bring into her day glimpses of You that encourage her. In Jesus name. Amen.

> Hi there. thinking about you with the bone scan today and hoping for answers!

> I spent a couple days in the hospital after entering ER with numb arm which lasted 10+ minutes. They still don't know what happened, but assuming mini either stroke or seizure or tickle of radiated brain metastasis spot or plain inflammation. Still investigating with tests next week. EEG. MRI. I was feeling back to my normal after 1/2 hour, so we shall see. They will probably cancel my next scheduled chemo until this gets figured out.

WOW! Lord, guide the doctors and technicians to find what they need to find in Cathy. Continue to hold her in Your peace. Give her strength, rest, and patience. In Jesus name. Amen.

> Scans are done. I won't hear anything until all the doctors read the scans. I'm hoping to know something by Monday at the latest.

Lord, continue to walk alongside Cathy as You have been. Make Your presence known to her today in some way. Thank You for all You are doing in her life. Help the medical people find answers to this latest unknown. Allow Cathy to rest in your arms, knowing that you are in complete control. In Jesus name. Amen.

Father, thank You for the medical community and all that it does for us.
Thank You for watching over Cathy and her entire family. Keep them safe and help them enjoy each other. Continue to bring answers to the medical challenges that come her way. In Your time, we know that healing does come. Thank You. In Jesus name. Amen.

Lord God, help us to worship You today. You alone are worthy of praise and worship. Help us to keep our eyes on You. Continue to direct Cathy and her medical team to answers and proper treatment. Help her in times of discouragement to know that you are right there with her. Bless her and her family as they rest in You. In Jesus name. Amen.

Father, thank You for Your constant, tender care of us. Thank You that You are always with us, no matter what gets thrown at us. Your presence gives us security and comfort, peace and joy. Extend these strongly to Cathy today. Bless her mightily. In Jesus name. Amen.

Lord, thank you for watching over and caring for us. Praise You for all Your creation and the joy You bring us in it all. Be with Cathy and guide and direct all that she does. Thank You for blessing her with Your grace and presence. Be with her in all she does today. In Jesus name. Amen.

Lord, thank You for the blessing of rest that you give us. Thank You for a fresh start every new day. Most of all Thank You for being right here with us in it all. Continued to be right there with Cathy, in it all. Bless her with rest and with You today. Continue the healing Lord. In Jesus name. Amen.

> How is it going with the knee?

Still in waiting purgatory. The doc needs to see the scans themselves, but the scan place is not know for speed in getting these things out. So I'm waiting

AND I didn't get a super power from the radioactive injection!

> If you can get on the online portal, let your doctor know that you saw the results and are awaiting his interpretation. Sometimes they need a little tickle. Sounds complicated And painful. I like your analogy with purgatory. I've been there a few times myself. I will say that I had an EEG yesterday and got the results online yesterday and from my doctor. It was normal. I have an MRI tomorrow. Then we go on vacation to Ocean City with my boys and sisters and families. Then CT. We skipped chemo this time until we figure out what is going on with my brain. When I get back from vacation the doctor said we will continue chemo.
>
> If radiation gave us a super power, people better watch out for me!

I did tell docs office I saw the results. And I called the scan place and put them on notice to get moving too. God's timing I guess. Waiting is not my strong point.

And YES if you got super powers the world would know it!

Heard from Dr. No surgery. Gotta stay off it as much as possible and use walker next 4 weeks. Check in with them weekly about progress. Said though things were lit up on the scans it didn't look like revision was needed. Yeah!

Wonderful news! Let the healing begin.

Father thank You for Your many blessings, the simple and the miraculous. Thank You for Your care through our this day as it unfolds for **us.** Be with Cathy and her family as they prepare to spend time together. Help them to enjoy each others company and may Your presence abound. In Jesus name. Amen.

Amen.

Lord, bless Cathy and her vacationing family with safety in travel and time away from home. Let them find places of joy and fun together. Grow their relationships even deeper. In Jesus name. Amen.

Father, as we go about our Sabbath day help us to rest in You as You have intended. Guide the joy and fun of Cathy and family. In Jesus name. Amen

Lord, thank You for Your everlasting love. You loved us when we were unlovable. We love you because you first loved us. Help us today to love like You. Give Cathy continued grace and mercy, rest and renewal. In Jesus name. Amen.

Lord, thank you for friends both near and far. Continue to give Cathy the energy and rest she needs. Prepare her for some super fun times with her family while they are away. Bless all of them to overflowing! In Jesus name. Amen.

Amen

Lord, continue to guide and direct the medical people in Cathy's life. Continue to bring health and healing. We trust in You for this and all things. You are God over all. Bring joy and happiness as family gather to celebrate live and life. In Jesus name. Amen.

Father thank You for being with us in times of uncertainty. Thank You for being our sure Rock that never waivers. Thank You for those who help take care of us when we can't ourselves (especially hubbies). Continue Your work in our bodies and spirits. Bring Cathy and family joy and rest, refreshment and laughter. In Jesus name. Amen.

Father, thank you for surrounding us with people that love us. Bring joy and more love to Cathy and her family. Keep the laughter and live flowing. In Jesus name. Amen.

Father, as we Sabbath today, let us honor You in all that we do. Whether it be in rest, enjoying friends and family, sharing food, or just having fun. Thank You for the continued ways to experience You. Bless Cathy and family today by drawing them closer to you and each other. May they make wonderful memories. In Jesus name. Amen.

Lord, thank you for the joys of this day. Thank You for the connections made and the laughter shared. You have been so faithful to show us Yourself in all of these things. Help us to see you in them as we review our day. In Jesus name. Amen.

Father, as we close this part of our day, we lift up to you our gratitude for all that you provided within it. For the laughter and connection to people we love. For the joy of companionship. For the rest experienced sprinkled in too. We are humbled by Your great care for us. Continue please to bless Cathy with all these things and with healing continued too. In Jesus name. Amen.

Lord thank you for a peaceful nights rest in your arms. Thank You for the things set before us today. People to meet and love. Help to give. Life to share. Bless Cathy and family today with amazing things. Shine Your light on them and let them experience Your grace today. In Jesus name. Amen.

Father, thank You for understanding friends who see our needs and help us meet them. Give us the grace to accept the help offered. Continue to strengthen Cathy and draw her closer to You. Bring Your presence into her day today. In everything we give You praise. In Jesus name. Amen.

Lord bring wonderful rest to Cathy this night. Bless her with gentle dreams in your arms. Bless her family with peace in You. In Jesus name. Amen.

Father, thank You for life giving food, and for fun food, like chocolate. You set our bodies into motion and know exactly what we need and enjoy. Thank You that you love us and care about the little pleasures in our lives. Help us today not to miss the little things You put in our day that make us smile. Work Your wonders in Cathy's life and body.
In Jesus name. Amen.

Lord God, thank You for the power You have over everything. You control the night and the day. Thank You for Your blessing us with both the night for rest and the day for encountering You. Bless Cathy with a fresh encounter of You today. In Jesus name. Amen.

Father thank You for Your patience with us. Thank You for giving us new opportunities to live according to your will and purpose. Thank You for loving us enough to cover our sins with the blood of Your Son. Thank You for all you are doing in and through Cathy. Bless her Lord, so that she can continue to be a blessing to others. In Jesus name. Amen.

Lord, thank You for Your Word. How it teaches us about your love for us and How we can love You better.
Thank You for the rain and the sunshine that you provide. Help us to see You in it all. Bless Cathy with the gentle rain of your grace as she draws nearer to You. In Jesus name. Amen.

Father, thank you for fun, laughter, friends (near and far), and family. Each is a blessing beyond measure. Thank You for what you are doing in Cathy's life. Thank You for the time she had with family and the memories they were able to make together. Continue to guide all of the medical people in her treatments. Help them to find answers and ways to help. In Jesus name. Amen.

Lord, Your blessings continually flow from Your Holy hands onto our lives. If *we were* to count them all, they would outnumber the leaves on the largest tree we see. Thank You. Be with Cathy. Strengthen her body, mind, and spirit with you and your ways. Let her know that she is never alone. In Jesus name. Amen.

Father, I ask that you continue to be near Cathy. Be her guide and supreme comfort. Help her to experience joy and laughter along with the questions, waiting and healing. Help her to continually rest in You. Thank You for being her hope and salvation. We love You Lord. Thank You for loving us. In Jesus name I pray. Amen.

Lord, thank you for the different ways that we get to worship and praise You. And not just on Sunday, but everyda*y*. As this day closes, bless Cathy with rest and joy. Guide her even deeper into You. In Jesus name. Amen.

God, thank you for the ways that you show us Your love. Through the words of a friend, the smile of a loved one or just the sunshine on the trees. Strengthen Your presence in Cathy's life, each day. Thank You for the ways You are bringing healing to her. In Jesus name. Amen.

Father, thank You for Your presence. How we are never without it. How it dwells within us. Your Spirit guides and gives us strength. Continue to guide Cathy and the medical personnel that are caring for her. Bless her with Your tender care. In Jesus name. Amen.

Lord God, open our eyes to Your Word today. Help us to hear from You through it. Bless Cathy with assurance of Your presence today. Comfort her and give her peace. Peace that passes all understanding. In Jesus name. Amen.

Father, You are so kind to us. Thank You for being with us and caring for our every need. Thank You for the strength to do the life things before us each day. Continue to be with Cathy and Mike as they grow together in You. In Jesus name. And.

Lord, thank You for Your mercy and grace. We don't deserve it, yet You pour both out on us everyday. Bless Cathy today with Your gentleness and grace abundant. Guide her decisions in ways that bring her peace. In Jesus name. Amen.

Father, thank you for the blessings that you have placed on our day. The ones we have already given and the ones yet to come. Bless Cathy and Mike with rest and time together today. Thank You for the life You give. In Jesus name. Amen.

Lord, thank You for being the covenant keeper. All of Your promises are true. Nothing can change what you are in motion. Thank You for all You are in Cathy's life. Continue to guide and direct and heal and reveal all that she needs. In Jesus name. Amen.

Father, thank you for the blessing of another day. Thank You for the people You have placed in our lives that we can minister to and who minister to us. Help us to be open to Your ways today. Bless Cathy with more rest and strength. In Jesus name. Amen.

Lord, another day is closing on us. As we look back on it help us to notice Your touch throughout it. Help us to see that you were right there with us in each moment. Easy moments and difficult moments. Give Cathy a wonderfully refreshing night's sleep. Let her awaken afresh to Your mercies tomorrow. In Jesus name. Amen.

> Amen. Back at you Miss Tammie

Father, thank You for the medical profession and you healing powers. Help us to rest in all that you have planned for us today. Give Cathy the strength and courage to continually lean into You. In
Jesus name. Amen.

Just returned from an unexpected knee doctor appointment. Had to have at swelling on my knee looked at again. They lanced it and PRESSED bunches of liquid out. Made a mess of the exam table. Took cultures. Stuffed it with gauze and wrapped it up. 2 more weeks of antibiotics. Rest and elevate. My Mom went with me.

> Wow. Sounds painful too. Will be praying.
> Glad you had Mom! Moms are the best!

Yes. Moms are great. She watched the whole thing. Gross.

> OMG! I could not watch. I am good for moral support

I couldn't watch. I was busy trying not to kick the PA who was doing the pressing and cutting....

> Exactly!!!

Father God, Ancient of Days, thank You for the day today. Thank You for helping hands and loving hearts. Thank You for laughter and joy. Thank You that in the midst of trouble and pain You are the ever present God. Bless Cathy with Your holy presence. Instill in her Your love and joy. Let her know that you delight in her. In Jesus name. Amen.

God, thank You for a fresh new day to stay in Your presence. Thank You for welcoming us into Your embrace. Let Cathy and Mike feel your loving arms surround them today. In Jesus name. Amen.

Lord, thank you for blessing us with another day. You give us mercy upon mercy and we can only say thank You. Continue to provide all the things that Cathy and Mike need. Rest, fun, laughter, strength, joy, family, and friends. Give them Your peace as they finish out this day with You. In Jesus name. Amen.

Father, help us to worship You today with the fullness of our hearts. Hear our praises as we worship You. Hear our prayers as we speak with You. Hear our hearts as we stand in Your presence. Guide Cathy in all that she does. Help her rest and know that you are with her. In Jesus name. Amen.

> Back at you dear Tammie.

Cultures came back as a Staph infection. They weren't sure if it was MRSA Or not yet. Those tests weren't in yet.

> Oh my! you are strong. You have been dealing with this a long time. Have they started you on an antibiotic yet?

I'm on 2 right now.

> Are they helping?

I just started them Wed. But I think they are.

> I know a little about MRSA from having a wrestling son. Some of his friends got it. I don't think you could have been walking around with it for so long. Scott's friends were very ill and hospitalized rather quickly. But then again, you are Tammie. Strong woman glad the antibiotics seem to be helping. Thankful

Thank you. There's a whole bunch I've learned lately.

> I bet. I had a lot to learn about cancer. You already knew about cancer unfortunately.

True

Father, guide Cathy in all that she says and does today. Let her know that you love her completely and unconditionally. Bless her with Your peace and joy. In Jesus name. Amen.

Infection identified as MSSA and not MRSA.

Father God, thank You for a new day. Thank You for Your great grace. Bless Cathy today, Lord, with gentle whispers from Your Word that she has hidden in her heart. Let her rejoice in each and every moment she spend with You. In Jesus name. Amen.

Lord, thank you for the power of rest. For the healing it brings to body, mind, and soul. Bring Cathy full rest today. In Jesus name. Amen.

> Glad you don't have MRSA. Have the antibiotics been doing their job? Feeling better?

I think things are getting better. I'm feeling better too.

> Wonderful. Praying for continuing progress.

Thank you!

Father, thank You for being with us each moment of each day. We couldn't do this without You. Thank You for keeping Cathy in the palm of Your mighty hand, where she is loved, safe, and eternally secure. Bless her today Lord, God with a deeper realization of that love and security. Thank You. In Jesus name. Amen.

Father, thank You for the sunshine through the trees today. Thank You for how Your Son shines in us each day. Bless Cathy and Mike with the shining of Your Son into their hearts and warm them in Your love. In Jesus name. Amen.

Lord, thank you for a night of rest and a new day to love you. We worship You and you alone God. You are the Maker of all. Thank You for crafting us. Bless Cathy and Mike today with time worshiping You together. Bless them with Your presence and love. In Jesus name. Amen.

Father, thanks for the hope that you bring with you very presence each and every day. Thank You for knowing each step we take and the safety we find in You each moment. Help us to be attentive to the still small voice that guides us. Bless Cathy with continued healing and strength as she continues along this path with You. In Jesus name. Amen.

Father, thank you for the patience of friends. Thank You for pouring Yourself out for us and then pouring Yourself into us. You are might to heal and it is healing that we constantly seek. Healing physically, emotionally, and spiritually. You meet us where we are and take us higher than we deserve. Bless Cathy with a most restful night sleep. In Jesus name. Amen.

Lord thank You for Your gentle care and comfort. You bring it through Your people to us, so thank You for them as well. Bless Cathy today with Your comfort and joy. In Jesus name. Amen.

Knee report from wound care Center: no wound vac! Derided existing hole. He cut another hole on the other side! Using Medihoney in the holes. Zinc oxide around the holes. Packing both holes now. See again next week. Don't bend knee too much. Now heading to ortho doc. Fun day.

> Wow, sounds painful. Prayers for you my dear.

Thank you

Father, thank You for the hunger and thirst you put into us to know more of You. Guide and direct Cathy as she seeks to dwell deeper in You. Bless her today with a deep sense of satisfaction in all that she is endeavoring to do. In Jesus name. Amen.

Lord, as we settle in for a night of sleep, Let us rest fully in You. Help us to remember that you do have everything in Your hands. In Jesus name. Amen.

Father, thank You for watching over us during the night as we slept. Refresh Cathy today as she moves through her day. Guide her into Your deep love in a fresh way. Continue to bring her healing and strength. In Jesus name. Amen.

> Back at you Ms. Tammie.

Father, You are wonderful, kind, and loving. You fill us with joy and hope as we trust in You each day. Bring Cathy Your unending joy as she goes through her day. Help her to see you in the many different moments of her day. In Jesus name. Amen.

> Wonderful. Amen. Same for you Miss Tammie!

Thank you.

Father, when we are discouraged, You lift us up. Thank You for Your neatness and care. Thank You that nothing that comes to us or from us surprises You. Yet, we are continuously and joyously surprised by You. Thank You. Bless Cathy with Your joy and a surprise or two. In Jesus Name. Amen.

Father, help us to see your fingerprints on the things that happen in our lives. Help us to be grateful and honoring to you in all things, good or bad. We praise Your name. I ask Father that you bring continued blessing so rest, healing, laughter, and joy to Cathy's life and to the lives of her family. In Jesus name. Amen.

Just saw wound care Dr. Both holes are looking good. I am now permitted to bend my knee moderately.

> Thankful!

Me too

> I bet!

Lord, You are our refuge and help, not just when we are in trouble, but all the time. Bless Cathy with Your mighty coverage and safety. In Jesus name. Amen.

> Amen. Always back at you dear friend.

Father, in the unexpected, You still remain true and sure. Your presence moves us through the unknown. Thank You. Bless Cathy with continued healing in Your presence. In Jesus name. Amen.

Lord, continue Your work in Cathy's life and the lives of her family. Draw them close to you and to each other. Continue healing and protecting her. Continue to help her live in Your presence. Surround her with You love today. In Jesus name. Amen.

On another note: I just got home from a trip to the ER per my wound care center recommendation. Looks like infection is back. They gave 2 antibiotic shots. Took X-rays and cultures. Awaiting lab results for specific antibiotics to kill this thing. Prescribed me 2 general ones to get things started. So I'm trying to rest and maybe get some reading done.

> I am so sorry Miss Tammie. I was just praying about the knee and was envisioning you bending the knee and it feeling better. More prayer I see. It sounds like you have a lot of medical people paying attention to you. Praying for patience for you and wisdom for the docs Hope you are feeling better soon.

Thank you so much

Father, thank you for the companions you bring to journey with us. Thank You for the wisdom You being us through them. Bless Cathy today, with a pouring into her Your holy wisdom. Help her to continue to grow into the beautiful princess You see her as. Help her to live out her identity as Your chosen child. In Jesus name. Amen.

> Amen. This is beautiful. Praying for you too. How is the knee?

Still spewing goop. But I think the antibiotics are starting to kick in. I am sure there will be a new one added once the test results of the cultures come in. Plus I'm hoping That the wound center will put me on a wound vac so I can stop messing with all the goop and changing to clean dressing and stuff.

> Oh my. Sounds nasty. Hopefully it will be clearing up soon.

I hope so too.

Lord, in the silence, let us hear You. We are thirsty for Your voice, and hungry for your touch. Thank You for what you are about to do in our lives. Bless Cathy with Your overwhelming, never-ending love. In Jesus name. Amen.

I cried out to the Lord, "God, come and save me!" He was so kind, so gracious to me. Because of his passion toward me, he made everything right and he restored me. So I've learned from my experience that God protects the vulnerable. For I was broken and brought low, but he answered me and came to my rescue! Now I can say to myself and to all, "Relax and rest, be confident and serene, for the Lord rewards fully those who simply trust in him." God has rescued my soul from death's fear and dried my eyes of many tears. He's kept my feet firmly on his path and strengthened me so that I may please him and walk before Yahweh in his fields of life. Even when it seems I'm surrounded by many liars and my own fears, and though I'm hurting in my suffering and trauma, I still stay faithful to God and speak words of faith. Psalms 116:4-11 TPT

I am choosing to lean hard into the last lines of where I am now.

> My dear Tammie. I am hurting when you are hurting. In my prayers I see you walking before Yahweh in his fields of life. In my vision, it is a big field with wildflowers. There, you are doing your works you were called to do and sharing the good news. I see you bringing Hope, smiles and joy to those around you like you do for me.

That is beautiful! Thank you my dear friend!

Father, bless Cathy today with a super around of sunshine to warm her and her world. And if it's cloudy or gray, pour more of Your love into her so that she herself shines out The Son and let her bask in Him. Thank You for Your grace and patience with us. In Jesus name. Amen.

Father, how blessed are we to be able to call you that, to be able to call out to you at all. You hear our smallest sighs to our loudest wails. And you love us gently into yourself. Hear Cathy today. Love her into You. In Jesus name. Amen.

Today's update: Wound care doc put a 3rd hole in my leg; extended a tunnel between it and the large hole: and ran a ribbon of Mesalt through it. Next week we might be able to put a vac on it. It's bleeding currently and they can't put one on if bleeding. I stubbed my baby toe and his neighbor on the wound leg the other day, but they are feeling better today. My right knee, the overworked one, is in excruciating pain. It does like to be straight, nor is it caring to be used to get from place to place. I found some left over Vicodin and am resting...as in, I'm actually in bed. And using the walker again.

> Oh dear. I was just praying about this matter. Did they identify the bacteria and start you on a new antibiotic? I am sorry for your troubles Dear Tammie.

Yes on antibiotics

> Well that's good.

Yeah.

I'm actually hoping next week, when they are done the wound doc will prescribe more

> I am glad you have a wound doc. They will know what to do hopefully. I will pray for wisdom for the that doctor.

Lord, bless Cathy and Mike today with Your gift of togetherness. Guide them into your healing presence. Comfort and meet their every need in You. In Jesus name..Amen.

Father, thank You for extra rest. Thank You for peace that God beyond expectations. Bless Cathy and Mike with extra rest and super peace today. In Jesus name. Amen.

Father, as this day draws to a close, we thank You for Your gentle closeness throughout it. Thank You for the assurances You give through Your Word. Help us to soak in Your Word daily. Bring Cathy rest, deep rest tonight. In Jesus name. Amen.

Father, thank You for You attention to the tiny details of us. Help us to pay attention to the tiny details of You overwhelming love and grace. Bless Cathy with an overabundance of the tiny things of You today. In Jesus name. Amen.

How are you miss Tammie?

I think things are getting better. The wound doesn't leak as much, but then again I put myself under house arrest and am not moving around all that much. The wound doc ordered a wound vac and I think he will show me how to use it on Friday when I see him next.

Sounds better anyway. Must be frustrating to be under house arrest and sitting still

It is. But I am learning stillness. And the beauty of it. And getting lots of reading done!

Well there is a lot you can do in stillness. Right, it's beautiful.

I don't know if you saw on caringbridge, but I have 2 new probable lesions in my brain. It's going to be a pain with my allergy to MRI contrast

Booger

Exactly

Lord go before and stand alongside. Be all around and bring peace to all. Steady hands and hearts. Your will be done. In Jesus name. Amen.

Wow, 2 in one day. Thank you. Amen and back at you my dear.

Gotta have extra in your back pocket!!!

Father, in the midst of life help us remain thankful. Help us to see the gifts You've given. The simple things. A flower. A leaf. The sound of a calm breeze on the water. The touch of a hand. Oh let us be always aware of your love and grace. Be with Cathy and bring her peace, Your wonderful peace, in all things. Walk beside her and keep her warm and full of joy. In Jesus name. Amen.

>> Amen and back at you

Lord, thank you for sunshine on a crisp fall day. Than You for the color of the leaves in the streams of that sunshine. Be with Cathy today. Be the light that shines onto her, in her, and out from her. Give her peace and rest. In Jesus name. Amen.

>> Amen.

Wound vac installed and running. Doc doesn't want to add antibiotic continuation so I don't become resistant or get a "raging" yeast infection. So we will go with that. Gotta keep the knee pretty straight, but I have no problem with that. The wounds themselves are getting smaller. Praise Jesus! I'm still limited, but healing. And am to keep the resting part going.

>> Sounds like progress. Thankful time to spend with Jesus and reading.

Absolutely!

Father, thank you for rest and hot showers inside warm houses. Thank You for surprise snow showers outside warm homes. Thank You for friends with warm hearts that care for us. Bless Cathy and Mike with the warmth of your presence in whatever they do. Accept their worship as a holy sacrifice and sanctify each of them with Your holy fire. In Jesus name. Amen.

>> Amen

Father, I pray that you will be with Cathy today. Hold her in Your warm loving arms. Gently guide her along this part of her journey of healing and love. Let her know that you are right there. That the questions she has are just the right ones and that you are answering them in the special way the two of you communicate together. Move the mountain before her. Level her path toward You. Be her rest and her peace as she walks in Your holy grace. Remind her that she is Yours. That You love her beyond that which any other can and there is nothing too hard for You. That she is safe with you as always. As You always do, Jesus, meet her right where she is and move with her in the direction of a deeper relationship with and in You. In Jesus name. Amen

>> Tammie, this is so lovely!!! Amen and Amen.

Lord, Your ways are too wonderful for our minds to fully grasp and understand. You bestow on us gifts that we don't deserve. Your love overwhelms us. Continue to bless Cathy today with your love and presence. Give her the strength to do that which You have prepared for her to do today. Let her find more of You in the stillness. In Jesus name. Amen.

>> Same for you my dear. Amen. Any improvement in the knee?

Thank you. I believe there is improvement. The wound vac is vac-ing and I'm still trying to be resting.

> Sounds good. Keep up the resting

Father, You have blessed us with a new day. Help us to see you today in a fresh way. Help us to know your presence is with us. Hold Cathy to Yourself and reveal to her today how special she is as Your daughter. Let her know that she is known by You and loved. In Jesus name. Amen.

Father, like a fresh wind, breath into Cathy renewed purpose and passion. Give her her heart's desire, as she seeks Your heart's desire.
Join with her in a powerful way today. In Jesus name. Amen.

Father, thank you for the highs and the lows of this week, You were in each. Thank You for the refreshment of Your Holy Spirit throughout this week. Thank You for times if stillness with Your Son. Help Cathy these times into her heart so that she can draw upon it as she needs to to pour out in the ways You have ordained for her. You have called her. She is Your chosen daughter. She is rock solid in You. Bless her as she continues this journey of healing. In Jesus name. Amen.

Father, our day closes and we thank You for Your presence in it. Thank You for Your word. Thank You for accepting our song and prayer to You this day. Give Cathy super natural rest tonight. In Jesus name. Amen.

Father, thank you that in the middle of uncertainty, You never change. We can be rock solid in who you are and always will be. Bless Cathy with Your certainty today. In Jesus name. Amen.

Lord, Your grace is sufficient for us. Help us to rest in Your sufficiently. Guide us in Your mighty love as only You can. Bless Cathy with continued rest and healing. Give her strength to do all that you have for her to do. Bring her comfort in the difficult times. In Jesus name. Amen.

> For you too

Thank you!

Father, thank You for Your presence. It is enough. Perfectly enough. Bless Cathy with an overwhelming sense of You today. In Jesus name. Amen.

I thought you might want to know this...Knee update: just got back from wound doc. Things are NOT good. The area under the hole is undermined in all directions. Think cave like. He says I can go to WI to visit Paul's family. Paul says we aren't, so we are staying in IN. Wound vac removed. Going back to packing and dressing it. Joy! He took cultures. Put me on an antibiotic. Wants me to see my knee surgeon ASAP. That appointment is set for

Monday at 9:50 am in his Indy office. So there you are. Updated. After the nurse got things cleaned up...it was messy this morning.....) and left the room. I did some deep breathing. A bit of crying. Then I asked Jesus where He was right then. He showed me that He was right there behind me, arms around me. Then He picked me up and carried me to a place by a window streaming with bright light.

> Tammie, I'm so glad that you let me know. I read this earlier, right before my walk and prayer time so it was great timing. You are certainly in my prayers my dear. It sounds like quite an ordeal and a very persistent infection! I pray Wisdom for your doctors in choosing the right antibiotic so that we can wipe out this infection! I'm sure it is very frustrating for you. It is marvelous when Jesus shows us himself! I just spent time reading And studying about Jesus in the garden of Gethsemane and then John chapter 18. I found a section of the BSF notes extremely meaningful. It's summarizes what I've been ruminating in my head that Jesus wants me to know and follow. I am praying along these lines. "God's light in the darkness. Jesus did not bemoan His circumstances. In loving obedience, He willingly carried out the will of the Father. Will your light shine in the darkness and bring glory to God? Will you deliberately choose to be conformed to His likeness by submitting to the circumstances of God's choice for you and triumphing in them in every detail, just as Jesus drank the cup His Father had given Him? Your witness is seen by others and cause them to know Christ, believe in Him and share in the eternal life the Lord Jesus Christ sacrificially has given you."

Thank you for that!

> Now, Jesus is certainly a tough act to follow, but he has given me direction, and he has given me himself. I am praying for courage to be able to use Jesus as my example of how to handle my adversity. As you witnessed today. Jesus walks everywhere with us!

I am following your example! God is in it all.

Father, help us to remain grateful and ever thankful, each and every day. Thank you Lord for all. Be with Cathy and family today. In Jesus name. Amen.

Father, thank You for family and friends. Thank You for provision and grace. Thank You for the example of faith You have given in Cathy. Bless her today with rest and healing and with the love of friends and family. In Jesus name. Amen.

I copied this prayer from a devotional on YouVersion Choosing Gratitude. "God, thank you for my Home Team. For those who come in without knocking and sit with me on my floor. Who tell me it's hard, it's ridiculous, it's over the top. Who give life to me simply by who they are and where *we*'ve been and what their grit and fight have been. Thank you for friendships that feel like siblings and love that feels safe and hilarious and easy. Thank you for those who are just so easy for us." Thank You God that Cathy is a member of my Home Team!. Amen.

> Aww. Thanks Tammie. This is great. I thank God that you are on my home team too!!! Hope you and Paul had a nice Thanksgiving.

Lord, God, at the end of this day we raise our eyes and hearts to You in thanks for Your work in it. Thank You for the blessings of family and friends. We thank You for the movements filled with laughter and the movements filled with quiet. In each one we can find You. Bless Cathy this night with restful sleep and peaceful dreams. In Jesus name. Amen.

Lord, thank You for Your Word and our ability to worship You freely. Hear our praise. Accept our worship. Bless Cathy today with a knowing that You hear her and love her. In Jesus name. Amen

Father, on this new day, we bring our praise to you. Thank You for watching over us and guiding us. Be with Cathy and guide her. Bring her rest and joy today. In Jesus name. Amen.

Here's the scoop on today's Dr appointment. He put a total of 3 needles in my knee, (the 1st one wasn't long enough, the 3rd was in a different spot for a different angle) to draw off some fluid for testing. He didn't get any. Not really a good thing. Not really a bad thing. Could mean its leaking out my wound, which is not good. Or could mean all is ok. He want to do a dye test to see for sure. So when he gets the dye (it's a blue dye) he wants he will call and arrange for me to have him again put a needle in my knee and insert the dye and see if it exits out the wound. If it does I'll probably head to surgery for an internal debridement & he will also check the actual hardware in there to see if it has been compromised with infection. He had me do some blood draws for testing. AND praise Jesus, he ordered me more than 2 weeks of antibiotics! He is setting me up with enough for 3 months!! I have a call into the director of my spiritual director @ options. My family and other non medical persons in my life think that it would be best to rest & not travel to 2nd residency for next week. I on the other hand believe that it's not out of the realm of possibility for me to continue as scheduled. I don't know exactly what to do. So I'm praying for clarity.

> I will pray too. Sounds like a long painful saga my dear. Will be praying for all of it.
> My PET scan is Thursday.
> It's nice that you have people that care about you even if you don't necessarily agree with all advice.

Praise Jesus it hasn't been very painful. I will be especially praying on Thursday then.

> Thanks Tammie!

I know they care. I just hate to have my plans messed with.

> Don't we all.

If I can pause the program and rejoin next year then I most likely will.

                Sounds reasonable. I vote with you, whatever you decide.

Nice

                Praying for clarity so you and Jesus want the same thing.

AMEN!

I have requested a pause in my Spiritual Direction program.

                Looks like you got clarity quickly. God has something else planned. You are always spiritually helping me and I am sure others. I am sorry you had to pause. I am sure that is disappointing for now.

God has a reason for it. I'm okay with it. Not my plan, but His. So much better way to live.

Yes

Interesting timing. Working on my BSF study lesson and read this in relation to the man left down through the roof by his friends: "Jesus dealt with a spiritual need that far exceeded the man's physical need." This is what He has been doing with me! Meeting the spiritual need before the physical one!

Father God You are ever faithful. You bring peace when we are at unrest.
You bring joy in sorrow. You delight in each of our moments spent with You. Bless Cathy with a full night of rest. Calm her mind as she sleeps, resting in You. In Jesus name. Amen.

 Father, go before Cathy. Prepare the way to a clear test tomorrow. Let the results be simple and small. Be with the medical persons that will be caring for her. Prepare Cathy with rest and peace. Let Your light shine through it all. Thank You for all you are doing in Cathy's life. In Jesus name. Amen.

Father, be extra close to Cathy today. Calm any nervousness and bring Your peace. Let Cathy experience Your presence in a real way today. In Jesus name. Amen.

 Father, bring Your overpowering rest to Cathy. Bless her with Your peace. In Jesus name. Amen.

Just spoke with knee surgeon. Going to have surgery next Friday. Debride, test with dye, clean all up and possible remove hardware if indicated. IV antibiotics after. Then oral antibiotics for life.

                Oh my goodness. Prayers for you miss Tammie. just this minute read my Pet results. Looks like I

> have a new lymph node in the neck and a spot or a few spots in my hip. Just digesting this now. I haven't heard from the doctor yet. Just reading this online.

Gotta love online access....

> Right. I was happier when I knew nothing.

I SO understand that!

The Christian does not think God will love us because we are good, but that God will make us good because He loves us. — C.S. Lewis

Father thank You for that outrageous love. The love that saw us as we were and gave Your Son's life to bring us back to you. Thank You for the work You do in us everyday. I ask that you bring peace to Cathy today. That she would be able to sense and feel your presence with her in a powerful way. Flood her soul with Your love and grace. Ease her mind. Help her to move through her day moment by moment experiencing You. Thank You for her example of grace. In Jesus name. Amen

> Beautiful! Thank you! Your surgery is the 10th?

Tea the 10th

Not tea, yes

> Oh gosh! I would love to have tea with you on the 10th! It sounds so much better than what either of us planned for that day. On December 10 I am going to Memorial Sloan Kettering in New York for another second opinion. It'll be a really long drive for Mike and me. A lot of time for bonding.

Yes tea would be better for both of us.

Father, I ask as Cathy and Mike prepare for this upcoming travel that Your peace would reign. That they would know Your provision and grace even now. That the roads would be clear and easy to navigate. And that the medical stuff be made clear. Bless Cathy with rest and Your mercy. In Jesus name. Amen.

Father thank You for Your timing in all that you do for us and allow into our lives. As Cathy prepares for this trip for another opinion, be with her and Mike. Let them rest in You and let your peace overwhelm them. Give wisdom to the medical people. Give them eyes to see what is there and minds to know what the next best steps will be. Give Cathy rest as she prepares for the long drive. In Jesus name. Amen.

Father, let your holy peace reign in Cathy and Mike. Prepare them for the drive on Friday and for the tests to be done. Remind them of Your presence with them each moment of the day. Thank You that with You, we are never alone. In Jesus name. Amen.

> Tammie, I am praying for your upcoming surgery. Lord Please give wisdom to these doctors so they know just what to take out and leave in for Tammie and her knee. We pray for peace which surpasses all understanding to be with Tammie and her family during this time.

Thank you!!!

Lord God, Creator of all, be extra close to Cathy today. Still her heart and mind to hear Your gentle whispers of love. Hold her gently but firmly in Your holy arms. Reassure her when she doubts of your presence and unending love and care. You are our only hope. We rejoice in knowing that this is all in Your hands. Thank you Lord for the mighty work You are going to do. In Jesus name. Amen.

Surgery is at 8 AM. Gotta arrive at the hospital at 5:45 AM.

> Wow. Prayers for you my sister.

Out of surgery and recovery. In hospital room at least overnight. Feeling good. Knee is immobilized in big brace. Haven't seen doc about all he did yet. Awaiting food! I'm hungry!

> Glad to hear from you! Hope the doc has good news. We are in waiting room. Haven't seen doc yet.

He just replaced the plastic spacer! No other replacement on this leg!

> Fabulous, right? Happy dance and praises!!!!

Lord, bring clarity and peace, wisdom and Understanding. Bless Cathy and Mike with Your presence. In Jesus name. Amen.

> Looks like MSK has a very encouraging clinical trial for me that I should qualify for. If so, we will most probably do it. Less side effects and will be in pill form within a few months. It will target my cancer mutation. This is very good news. We are very thankful. How are you?

Praise Jesus!

I'm really good!

> Thankful for so much today

Me too!

They are culturing my bugs to match best antibiotics for me to be the next 8 weeks. Should be putting in pic line today. Doc assistant said cultures should be in by Monday so I'm thinking I'll be here til then.

> Oh. Sorry to hear about the longer stay. But we need the best antibiotics! Lots of prayer time and Bible study time. And watch a nice movie. Is Paul visiting a lot or does Covid prevent that? Praying for wisdom for everyone involved in testing and choosing that antibiotic

Lord, Thank You for opportunities that are available to us medically that haven't been before. Thank You for Your grace and mercy toward us. You are an amazing God and may we never cease to be in awe of You. Bless Cathy and Mike today with rest and quietness of surroundings. Renew their physical and spiritual strength. Bless them with Yourself. In Jesus name..Amen.

Paul is on his way to visit and Mom too! Right now just masking when out in halls and such

> And you can tell people at the hospital about your Jesus. Every time tried at HOCO general, people were believers and we had the most wonderful spiritual conversations.

The hospital here seems to be full of faith people. Had God conversation with blood draw person at 5 am this day.

> Yes. People in medical services. Makes sense.

Father, continue Your healing work in Cathy. Continue to bring her rest and peace in body, mind and spirit. She knows she is in Your Almighty hands. Hold her gently to your heart and bless her with a night of peaceful rest. In Jesus name. Amen.

Father, You are almighty and in total control of all that is in our lives. Thank You for watching over Cathy and guiding her care. Bless her with the assurance of You. In Jesus name. Amen.

Looks like I'll be going home later today.

> Wonderful news! I have an echo cardiogram at one. I have a lot of tests to pass before I can get the trial drug. I'm sure being home will be wonderful for you! I know the hospital is like being in the cage after a couple days. Thankful for your release!

Doc said the infection was from outside in instead of other way which is a good thing.

Lord, as we begin our day, we worship You. We thank you for the mercies and grace that you have in store for us today. I as that you bring healing to Cathy's body, mind and spirit. That Your Holy Spirit be at powerful work in her as she awaits the next medical steps. Grant her continued peace and rest. In Jesus name. Amen.

Father, we praise You for who you are. No other reason is necessary. We thank you in advance for the mercies of this day. Bless Cathy with
extra time in Your holy presence. Remind her that she is in Your loving care. That You see all that is happening. In Jesus name. Amen.

Lord, let today be a day of simply rejoicing in You, in all You are and in all You have done. Guide us with Your Holy Spirit into your heavenly courts to praise You. Be with Cathy as she praises You. Guide her day. Bless her with Your delight in her. In Jesus name. Amen.

Father, be Cathy's rest tonight. Strengthen her hope in You. Bless her with deep, restful sleep. In Jesus name. Amen.

Lord thank You for rest and worship. we worship You Lord God for Your wonderfulness toward us each and every moment of each day we take breath. Help us to remember that we owe our every breath to You. You love us and guide us each day. Help us listen to your still voice of peace and enjoy You today. Bless Cathy today with ease of breath. In Jesus name. Amen.

Father thank You for wisdom and guidance. Thank You for caring and loving friends and family. Thank You for the precious gift of Your Son. Guide us this week in the light of Your love and this day in the glory of Your grace. Bless Cathy with peace and rest as she prepares her heart and home for Your Son's birthday celebration. Give her strength. In Jesus name. Amen.

Father, give your strength for the battle to Cathy today. Help her to walk in Your love and grace as her covering of protection. Let her rest in full surrender. In Jesus name. Amen.

These are precious prayer. Back at you my friend.

Thanks

Father, even when life seems difficult or even scary, You are here in it with is. You never leave our side. We are never alone. Bless Cathy with the assurance of Your love and presence. Hold her to Yourself. Remind her she isn't alone. Bring peace and rest to her throughout this day and the days that follow. Help her to celebrate Your birth with thanksgiving and joy. In Jesus name. Amen.

Staples out! No more poking at me when I put the brace thingy on! All that is left to come out now is a few stitches that he used to close up the wound hole in a couple of weeks. Much more comfortable now. Mom and sister took me out to lunch before my appointment so its been a long day for me. I am beat, but oh so upbeat with my Jesus!

Lord, help us to lean into You in all things, good and not so good. Here in You we find peace that passes understanding. Help us to not resist Your use of the negative in our lives so that we don't miss a deeper way into your love and grace. Help us go deeper. Help us hear Your voice and feel your love and presence. Keep Cathy in Your holy hands. Love on her especially hard today. In Jesus name. Amen.

> So happy about your good news and that you are feeling better! Just in time to marvel and praise at our Saviors birth! Quite a lot going on here, we will be traveling to New York's Memorial Sloan Kettering to see if I can participate in a trial. The trail drug would specifically target the mutation of cancer that I have and spare me a lot of chemo side effects. The doctor seems to think it is a great drug. Sorry if I'm repeating myself we will leave on 4 January for tests on the fifth and sixth. I won't find out about the trial until January 10. Then the new drug would be administered on the 11th. All that being said, I could not receive the trial drug but another chemo. Obviously we are hoping for the trial drug. And we are hoping to be accepted into the trial. But even if we are not....... I guess you know the rest.

I will be praying

> Daniel three verses 17 and 18.

> Your prayers are beautiful my dear. Thank you immensely!

> My son is sick in Pennsylvania, so he will not be coming for Christmas. My son in Colorado is not coming either. I think they are concerned about my lung scarring and trying to keep me safe. Looks like it will be Christmas for two with an 18 pound turkey

Lots of leftovers! Yeah!

Father on this eve of the day we celebrate the birth of Your Son, give joy to hearts all around us. Yet don't let us forget the very purpose of His birth. Let that deepen our joy and celebration. Be with Cathy as she anticipates a quiet Christmas and the upcoming drug trial. Keep her in your continued peace. In Jesus name. Amen.

Merry Christmas. Lord, bless Cathy and Mike today with your love as they celebrate Your Son's birth. Let them rest in your complete care. In Jesus name. Amen.

> And Tammie and Paul. Amen. Merry Christmas my dear.

Father, thank you for the greatest gift ever, Jesus. Thank You for wanting to walk with us in our lives. Bless Cathy today with rest and peace. Assured in the knowledge that You walk with her now. In Jesus name. Amen.

Lord, thank you that you have everything under your control. That You see us and care for us. Let Cathy know deeply of Your love and care. That she is seen and not overlooked. Watch over her and Mike as they prepare to travel. Open just the right medical path for them. Bless them with certain peace that they are right where You need and want them to be, the very palm of your hand. In Jesus name. Amen

Lord, as anxiety rises about the upcoming drug trial trip, I ask that your peace would overwhelm Cathy instead. Let her know that she is in Your care and nothing happens without Your hands touching it. Bless Cathy today with Your strength and resolve. We love You Lord and place all of who we are and ever will be into your hands. In Jesus name. Amen.

> Thank you Tammie!!! There is just a little anxiety. More over not getting in the trial or not getting the trial drug. But even if...... I know God is with me and working out all the details.
>
> How is the knee?

The knee is doing good. Stay in His care my friend.

Father, thank You for Your constant nearness to us. Thank You that you are putting all the details on place for the "whatever's" in our lives. Help Cathy and Mike rest in their whatever's. Ease minds and hearts and help them to walk through this time of anxiety, big or small. Show Yourself to them in special ways today. In Jesus name. Amen.

> Amen

Father, as we look back and consider the year behind and look forward and consider the year to come, we can't but help to give You praise. You have had us in Your hands, even when we didn't sense it. And because You are an unchanging God, we can know that our next year will be the same, ever in Your hands. And quite frankly Father that is more than enough, and more than what we deserve. Help Cathy to continually know deep and firmly that she is Your valued princess and ever in Your care. Regardless of what is too come, we say, "and if not, He is still good." Help us remain anchored in that. In Jesus name. Amen.

> Amen.

Father, thank you for the days of this year passing. Thank You for the days You are about to walk with us in. We trust you in what you have prepared for us. Help Cathy to continually hold onto your hand as she steps into the new year and the new medical treatment. Help her be continuously reminded of Your presence with her each moment. When she is afraid, hold her close. When she is unsure, stand beside her and hold her up. Bless her with peace and super rest. In Jesus name. Amen.

> Beautiful. Back at you friend! Happy New Year!

Father, help us to begin our new year solidly resting on Your will and care. Let the foundation You are in our lives grow stronger and let us root deeper in You. Bless Cathy with continued peace. In Jesus name. Amen.

> Hi there. Like the "us" in your prayer today. Tammie, Cathy and our loved ones. My mother is struggling the last week. She is probably in her last few days of severe dementia until she is with Jesus and in his arms for eternity. Love my mama

I'm sorry to hear that your Mom is going, but I hear in your words that she will soon be whole and rejoicing. That is a comfort in sure.

Father, it is in You that we rejoice. We praise Your holy name. Thank You for granting us another day to offer you our praise. Praise for things You have done. Praise for what you are doing. And praise for what you are going to do. Guide and direct Cathy into.a deep, deep place of peace about the trip this week. Prepare the way. Settle hearts and minds into your holy plan for her. Give her and Mike rest in the next several days. In Jesus name. Amen.

> Mom is in heaven as of 3pm.

I'm so sorry. May you be comforted by God's hand and grace.

Father, in this time of sorrow, be overwhelming comfort. Bless Cathy and her family with Your grace and comfort. Be with Cathy and Mike as they get ready for travel to see about a new treatment possibility. Give wisdom and discernment to the medical staff. Bless Cathy with continued awareness of You. In Jesus name. Amen.

> Mike and I are in our way. Just prayed this together with our prayers

Father, as the journey continues do Cathy and Mike to a different and new treatment, watch over them. Keep them safe. Help them to get rest. Help them remain in You ad You remain in them. Guide the medical persons with Your will for Cathy and the cancer. Give the wisdom and disc that can only come from You. Keep Cathy and Mike fully in Your peace no matter what the outcome. In Jesus name. Amen.

Father, continue to walk closely with Cathy and Mike. Give the extraordinary peace. Peace that only comes from You. Bless them with that peace from head to toe. In Jesus name. Amen.

Lord, the options we had hoped for have turned a different way. *We* rejoice in no growth of cancer, but mourn the treatment that we had hoped for. Hold Cathy especially close in this part of her journey right now. You are our Healer and we place her in Your total care. Give her and Mike a peaceful journey back to their home. Give them needed rest. In Jesus name. Amen.

Habakkuk 3:17-19

>Yes!

Father as this day closes, help us look back and see the little places You were with is. Draw Cathy to Yourself. Give her rest and peace of mind. In Jesus name. Amen.

Lord, on this day of rest, give Cathy and Mike rest. Rest beyond a physical rest that can only be from You. Let that rest be worship to You. Continue to reign peace in their lives and home. In Jesus name. Amen.

Father, we rejoice in another day to walk with You here. We couldn't do this life without You. Thank You for each step You take with us, though sometimes we may not be aware of You in it. Make us more aware of You in each moment today. Bless Cathy with the awareness that you are aware of her. You see her. You are right there with her. Help her to mourn what needs to be mourned freely with You. Let her know that no of it surprises You. In Jesus name. Amen.

>So spot on my dear. Thank you!!!!

God knows!

Lord, God of all, You are amazing and we praise You. In the midst of crazy, You are present. In the peace and calm, You are there. Help us to see You when things both go our way and don't go our way. Help us to make Your way, our way. Bless Cathy as she adjusts to the passing of her Mom. Fill her with Your peace as she rest assured that her Mom is with You. Bless Cathy today with recovering rest, body, mind, and spirit. In Jesus name. Amen.

Father, reign in us. Be the strength of our day. Be the peace in our life. Send sweet whispers of love and assurance to Cathy through this day. Remind her of Your love and presence with her. Hold her in her grief and her joys. Let her be aware of you. Help her to let go of what isn't of eternal value and fully focus on that which is. In Jesus name. Amen.

Father, thank You for the grace and mercy to begin another day with You. Thank You for watching over us through the night. Continue to wrap Cathy close in Your arms. Guide the decisions that she needs to make today. Let Your love shine into her and be her ever guiding light. Reminder her that she is not alone. In Jesus name. Amen.

>Thanks Tammie. Sitting at JHU waiting for the lymph node biopsy. How is the knee?

The knee is progressing. I'll be off the IV antibiotic next Friday and hopefully the immobilizer too. Then the fun of PT and bending will happen.

Lord, guide all that is happening with Cathy this moment. Guide the doctors and nurses and other medical staff. Give Cathy peace in the outcome. We rest in You and trust the path You have us on. Hold Cathy close. In Jesus mighty name. Amen.

Father, thank You for Your care. It is constant and everlasting. Give Cathy rest and peace of mind today. Be with her and let her know that there is not one emotion that pushes You a away. You are her rock. In You she is strong. Thank You Lord. In Jesus name. Amen

> Glad the knee is progressing will pray that PT goes well. Thank you for the prayers which cover both of us.

Father, thank you for the light You give us to carry to our world. Thank You for using Cathy to take the Kingdom of Heaven to places that need to see and experience Your love and life. The path she is on isn't what she would have chosen, but Your Light is going out into places that she goes. Continue to give her strength to do what you have set for her to do. Bless her with peace and rest. Give her Your blessed hope. In Jesus name. Amen.

Father, thank you for the beauty we see all around us when we pause to look. Thank you for the strength You have prepared for us to draw upon today. Thank You for walking with Cathy. For loving on her in many unique ways. Give her a song for her heart to sing today. Bless her as she praises You despite the circumstances. In Jesus name. Amen.

Song to listen to: <u>Take Heart</u> by Mission House
https://m.youtube.com/watch?v=VM56MmZHk-U

Father, thank You for Your continued grace in our lives. Thank You for Your guidance. Bless Cathy today with calm and peace inside and out. Let nothing shake her. Help her to hold fast to You. In Jesus name. Amen.

Lord, thank you for who you are in each moment to us. I ask that you would be with Cathy in a powerful way today. Let her feel Your holy presence. Let her hear You singing over her in love. In Jesus name. Amen.

Lord God, You are all for us. You cheer for us and weep with us. Our joy is Your joy. Help us to make Your joy our own. Help us hold fast to You no matter what. Thank You for all you do in our lives, especially the things we are presently unaware of. Bless Cathy today with the awareness that You fully see her right where she is and You live her just as she is. Put a blanket of comfort about her. In Jesus name. Amen.

Father God, thank you for every beat of our heart and every breath we take. You know each one and are the Author of them all. Be with Cathy today and bring her deep rest and calm. Remind her of Your knowing her inside and out and that nothing happens in her that surprises You. And that nothing can separate her from You. In Jesus name. Amen.

> Hi there friend. My lymph node biopsy showed cancer. I haven't spoken with the doctor yet but she expected theses results.

I'm sad to know that it was what was expected. But it didn't surprise God. Let Him love on you today however He wants.

I'm permitted to start bending my knee!!!

> Woo hoo! Thankful!

Father we praise You for the energy to do the things we did in our day today. Thank You for blessing us today with laughter and tears, and friends and family. Watch over and bless Cathy and Mike with rest and peace, in the midst of the good and the not so good. Hold them to Yourself and help them find ways to praise and worship You. In Jesus name. Amen.

Lord, You are holy and more than worthy of our worship and praise. Thank You for loving us and blessing us so beyond what we can imagine. Be with Cathy as she walks with the good and not so good on her path. Make her constantly aware that she is never alone. And when she is weary, Lord, help her rest in You and let you carry her. In Jesus name. Amen.

Father, praise Your name. You are the only true God. Your love is everlasting and your presence with us never goes away. Bless Cathy today with evidences of your presence. Let her see Your fingerprints all over her life - past, present, and future. Help her rest in You today. In Jesus name. Amen.

Father, we rejoice in all that you have provided for us in this day so far. We praise You ahead of time for all that you will be doing in the remainder of our day. Thank You for the every movement of our body. From the largest step we take to the smallest cell doing its work inside of us. Help us to see with Your eyes the life all around us and within us. Bless Cathy today with unencumbered movement in all things. In Jesus name. Amen

PIC line is out. I drove the hour up to the doctor, had breakfast (appointment was for 8:30 in the a of m) and drove the hour back. Mom was my sidekick today. And backup driver. I even did a few errands.

> Wow, real progress. It must feel good to be out and about!!! Thankful!

It really does!

Father, we reach to You in times of uncertainty, and You are there. *We* reach out in our pain and You are there. We reach out in our joy and You are there. You are always there, reaching toward us as *we* reach toward you. Continue to reach toward Cathy as she reaches toward you. Draw her close to your heart in all times and in all ways. Bless her today with the reachable-ness of You and hold her with You. In Jesus name. Amen.

Lord, it the quiet moments You can speak volumes to us. Let us seek the quiet moments. Thank You Father for all that you are doing in Cathy's life. You reign in her heart. Stay near her and guide her today. In Jesus name. Amen.

Father, You live abounds in Your children. Thank You for that love. Not just for myself to hold onto, but to share with others. As Cathy continues this journey, keep her full to overflowing with Your love, as she gives it out to those that she encounters. Bless her with peace and deep rest. In Jesus name. Amen.

Lord, You have blessed us beyond anything we deserve. Thank You, seems like such a weak response to what you have done for us and in us, but it is all we can say right now in this mortal form. Thank You. Thank You. Thank You. We lift our hearts and praise You today, for the richness of your presence with us. Be Cathy's guide and comforter today. Step beside her in her day and be with her in a strong way. In Jesus name. Amen.

> These beautiful prayers are really speaking to me. Thank you Jesus for speaking through my friend.

Blessings upon blessings be yours today.

> And yours my friend!

Father, we worship You. We give you our praise. You alone are worthy. You are in all that surrounds us and You reside within us. Hold Cathy in Your embrace as she worships You. Sing sweetly over her a song just for her. In Jesus name. Amen.

God, Your love is a banner of victory over us. You have already won the entire war and stand with us in the battles we daily fight. Help us to rest in the knowledge that in You we have won too. Bless Cathy today with a glimpse of Your banner of victory over her and the battles she fights. Give her super assurance that she wins with You every day. In Jesus name. Amen.

> The banner of victory is especially great today!!! Back at you dear Tammie!

God, You are our Sustainer. You provide everything we need. You even provide Yourself to us to sustain us each day. You nurture and care for us, gently like a mother does her child. Be Cathy's Sustainer and provider today. Gently care for her and nurture her spirit and body. Bring Your strength to her today. In Jesus name. Amen.

Father, it is amazing how you meet us in each of our different needs and moments. You are with Cathy right now and in every moment that comes and each one that has past. Bless her with an overwhelming presence of Your Holy Spirit today. And a sure knowing that you truly are in every moment and in every breath she breathes. In Jesus name. Amen.

Lord, we are blessed to be Your children, Your servants. You are holy and true and You love us with an amazing, everlasting love. Help us not to lose sight of Your love for us. Bless Cathy today with the stillness of your presence. Let that stillness sink deep within her. Let her rest there with You, letting everything else go. In Jesus name. Amen.

God, You are awesome, almighty, strong and powerful. You are God and to be awed and feared. Yet we are blessed to call You Father and Friend. How amazingly, wonderful is that?! Thank You for Your mercy, grace and love. In the stillness of this evening reach down and bless Cathy with Your love and grace. Hold her and give her rest. In Jesus name. Amen

Lord, we close another day in which You have been with us. You are with Cathy in the disappointment, pain, and struggle, we know that. We also know that there is joy, laughter, and rest in her journey. Help Cathy to focus on Your face in the good and not so good. Hold her tight when things go sideways and upside down. Be with her this night and give her amazing rest and sleep. In Jesus name. Amen.

God, as we settle into the night to go to sleep, we are reminded that you never sleep. You are always on duty, watching over us. Thank You. Thank You that you are with Cathy and with me at the same time. Watching over and caring for each of us in our different needs. Bless Cathy with extra ordinary sleep and rest tonight. Let her awaken afresh and anew tomorrow in Your almighty hands. In Jesus name. Amen.

Father, the sun had risen on a new day. You cared for us through another night. Bless Your holy name. Be with Cathy today. Guide her in all she does and thinks. Continue to draw her closer to your heart. In Jesus name. Amen.

Lord, You have overcome all. There is NOTHING that you can't handle. Nothing in our lives is too big or too small for you to take care of. And nothing surprises You. Thank You for loving us. Bless Cathy with the certainty that you have everything in her life under Your care for her ultimate good. In Jesus name. Amen

> Still no insurance approval for my radiation on Friday but I am at peace. It is still in the appeal process. I feel Jesus directing my steps. How is the knee "moving" along?

The knee is bending. I can sit in a chair with it bent nearly 90 degrees. Things are still swollen, but that can last rather long. I can get in the car and drive. No pain. So all in all doing very well.

Lord, You know what is best. So we place the radiation treatment and its cost in Your hands. It's the safest place for Cathy to stay so keep her at peace and fully resting in You. Bless her with resilience and strength as she walks this path with You. In Jesus name. Amen.

> Thankful you are progressing well. No pain is wonderful. Thanks for the prayers.

You are loved!

> Aww. You too my dear

Thanks!

Father, bless Cathy with a great nights rest in Your holy arms. Give her peace of mind about the treatment tomorrow. Let any concerns about insurance just slide away. You are in control. You see what lies ahead. Let her rest in You this might. In Jesus name. Amen.

Father, blessed be Your holy name. You are mighty and worthy of our praise. Be with Cathy in this treatment today. Give her the strength she needs. Give her rest afterwards. Be with the medical team treating her. Let them see you through her. In Jesus name. Amen.

> One of my two procedures has been approved. There's currently one pending. Very thankful Lord Jesus! I also have a new advocate at Johns Hopkins helping me navigate all of this. Thankful

Praise Jesus!

Father, thank you for the warmth of Your love that flow to us through Your Holy Spirit. Bless Cathy with rest and calm. Allow her to sense Your never ending love for her today in that rest and calm. In Jesus name. Amen.

Lord, thank you for the gift of another day. Thank You for keeping Cathy in Your tender care. Continue to bring her rest and peace. Bring her joy and laughter along with Your grace and love. In Jesus name. Amen.

Father, draw Cathy into your great loving kindness. Surround her with great peace and love. In Jesus name. Amen.

Thank You, Father, for the ability to come to you as a little child. Help us to come with the wonder and excitement of a child into your presence as often as we want. Shine the light of Your love on Cathy today. Allow her to see your smile today. In Jesus name. Amen.

Father thank You for the wonder that Cathy is, to You and to those who know her. She shines Your love. Thank You that you are with her and have no intentions on leaving her. She is never alone. Be with her today in Your marvelous way. Guide her and bring her peace. Draw her family, especially her boys, deeper into you. In Jesus name. Amen.

Father, You are all powerful but so gentle with us. We are Your children and You love us tenderly and greatly. Thank You. Bless Cathy today with a sense of that tender love. Let her know that You have her wrapped in Your loving, tender arms. In Jesus name. Amen.

> Tammie, if you look at your prayer for yesterday it was so appropriate. A huge blessing occurred yesterday. My son Mark brought his new girlfriend to our Bible study last night. This is huge. Thank you Jesus! My prayers are being answered. Additionally,

she speaks Spanish and so does Scott's girlfriend. I think God is going to work on that link and get Scott's girlfriend to Bible study too. I am so extremely grateful and this is a huge blessing! Thank you Jesus!!!

How is the knee? And how is Tammie?

God is SO amazing! My knee is progressing. I can drive so I am free! I am doing well. God continues to grow me and I don't fight too much...so progress there. He is stretching me.

No surprise with God stretching you. You have a lot of gifts and talents. He is just figuring out where to use them to bring him glory.

I like that. Thank you for that perspective.

You are welcome.

Father, we thank You for Your unfailing love. I thank You for Your care of Cathy and Your planned healing of her body. Though we don't know the form or the time, we trust that you will accomplish it all the same. Bless Cathy with reassurance of Your plan for her. In Jesus name. Amen.

Father, thank you for a fresh new day to worship You. Help us to worship You fully with all that is in us today and always. Be with Cathy and give her strength and peace. Continue to work in the hearts and lives of her boys. Draw them to You. Bless Cathy with a peace and reassurance that you are at work in them in ways that are amazing. In Jesus name. Amen.

Father thank you for your mercy and grace. Thank you Lord for the ways that you show Cathy your love continue to guide her and direct her continue to bring her hope. Let her know in some special way today that you have everything under control amidst the chaos and uncertainty. I asked these things in Jesus mighty name amen

You got it. Father, You are in control, not man. Work behind the scenes and put the plan in place that is perfect to fit Cathy. Yesterday is past and still a part of Your plan. Let today show Your sovereignty in a mighty way. Give Cathy Your peace in the midst. In Jesus name. Amen.

Thank you Tammie. You see how your prayer yesterday, was very needed. I saw it as I was waiting to find out why they pulled me off the cyberknife table. I was at peace and was able to share my peace and my God with the technicians. God has everything under control.

God loves you!

Thank you Lord! A plan has been finalized and they moved my appointment to 2:30.

Way to go God!

Father, You are amazing. You meet our needs before we even know we have them. Give Cathy rest and peace today that can only come from You. Draw her family into deeper relationship with You. In Jesus name. Amen.

Father, thank You for the safety that you give. Safety physically, emotionally and spiritually. Guide and direct Cathy today as she walks with You. Keep her safe and secure in Your love. Bless her with a great sense of You today. In Jesus name. Amen.

Lord, thank you for watching over Cathy. For giving her strength to do all that she does. We rejoice in another day that we get to spend with You. We thank you that you see each movement we make. That You provide each breath that we breathe. Help us to take time today and just breath in You. In Jesus name. Amen.

> Tammie, I finished my radiation yesterday but I'm having excruciating nerve pain as a side effect. Apparently the tumor was sitting on my nerve and it gets a little inflammation. I just started on some dexamethasone for inflammation. Thanks so much for the prayers!
>
> How is the knee?

Super. Healing well. Bending some better too

Father bring the richness of Yourself to Cathy in all she does today. Give her rest and joy. In Jesus name. Amen

> At emergency room. Pain meds. Anti-inflammatories.. Doing scans to check for structural damage.

Lord, give wisdom. Bring relief. Bring peace and rest. In the mighty name of Jesus. Amen.

Father, we worship You. We thank You for the medical help that is available to us. It is You who have provided this gift to us. I pray for continued pain relief for Cathy. Bless her with a quiet, peace filled day that she can rest. If there is anything in her body that needs attention, pray that it would be attended to quickly and completely. In Jesus name. Amen.

Father thank You for Your amazing grace. Thank You for meeting Cathy just exactly when, where, and how she needs to be met. Continue to give her pain relief. Comfort her and give her rest and peace throughout this day. In Jesus name. Amen.

Father, Your ways are beyond anything we can imagine. Bring us hope when all seems hopeless. Give us peace in unrest. Walk beside us when we feel so alone. Thank You for doing all this for Cathy. Continue to make her aware that You see her, love her, and are caring for her. In Jesus name. Amen.

Lord, thank You for Your almighty grace toward us. We so don't deserve one ounce of it. Thank You that you see us no matter where we are or what we are doing. Guide all that Cathy needs in Your grace. Bless her with continued relief and rest. Help her to hold onto You in the midst. In Jesus name. Amen.

Further God I thank you for the dawning of another day a day that we can worship you a day that we can find you in the midst of everything else that's going on in our lives. I asked that as you walk with Cathy today She would feel your peace She would know you are right there beside her. I asked that you would continue to bring her pain relief and that you would give her a mighty rest today I ask these things in Jesus name. Amen

Father of all, pour out Your Spirit overwhelmingly on Cathy today. Give her continued relief and super rest. Bless her with more of You. Bring her boys even closer to your heart. In Jesus name amen.

Father, as we worship You, hold the enemy at bay. Cancel his agenda as we praise You. You alone are worthy. Bless Cathy with Your overwhelming grace and peace as she rests in Your provision. In Jesus name. Amen.

Father, You are the giver of all gifts. You hold us in Your care day and night. Thank You for how You are moving in our lives and the lives of those we love. Move us closer to your heart with each beat. Bless Cathy with Your assurance that you have her and her family in the palm of your hand. Totally secure. In Jesus name. Amen

Paul got an appointment at the Headache Clinic! He is to be there March 28th! If he is admitted he will be there 7 to 10 days.

> Wow, so thankful for this path! Prayers for wisdom and insight for the doctors. Peace and progress for you and Paul. God has this!

Oh YES!

Lord, You know the path that we travel. You walk it with us. You provide companions to walk with us along the way. Thank You for meeting with us today. Bless Cathy with companions and comfort today. In Jesus name. Amen

Father, where you are there is love and peace. You desire above all relationship. Thank You that you want relationship with us. Increase the depth of Cathy's relationship with You. Guide here in Your love. In Jesus name. Amen.

Father You are great ad greatly to be praised. So, we lift up our praise to You and You alone. You are working in Cathy's life for her good and Your glory. Continue to walk with her and guide her. Work in her and through her. Thank You God. In Jesus name. Amen

Lord, You are our greatest hope. So we rest in You. We lay aside our cares and place them in Your hands. Let Cathy rest in Your care. Let no care overwhelm her. Be her security and future. Bring her boys deeper into your heart. In Jesus name. Amen

Father, You are ever so reliable. Nothing changes who you are. You are the all encompassing mighty ruler of the universe and beyond. You are greater than our fears. More wonderful than we can even begin to imagine. And You love us! How amazingly wonderful that is. Bless Cathy today with the wonderment of Your overwhelming love for her and her family. In Jesus name. Amen

God, You are holy and worthy of our praise. We praise You for You eternal goodness. No matter what is happening, we know that you are good and that you love us. Bless Cathy today with rest and a filling of Your goodness. In Jesus name. Amen

> Any improvement for Paul?

No. All is the same.

> Praying.

As you know, that's the best thing

> Best medicine!

Father, as the sun shines today we remember that Your Son reigns on high, over all. Thank You for rescuing us. Thank You for the Healing You have in store for Cathy. Bless her today with a taste of that healing. In Jesus name. Amen

Lord, watch over my friend Cathy today. Be her guide and comfort. Bring her peace in the midst of all the even if's. You are her God and she rests in You. Draw her boys deeper into You. In Jesus name. Amen

Father, thank You for Your protection. Thank You for being with Cathy. Continue to hold her and guide her. Continue to open healing doors for her. Bless her with rest today. Your rest and peace. In Jesus name. Amen

> For both of our families. Amen.

Yes

> I have not heard about the study yet. But I can see my scan results and it looks like I have no new brain lesions and no new metastasis. I also only have minimal growth in the lymph node which probably does not qualify me for the trial. I will wait to hear from the trial doctor hopefully tomorrow. So again this is very good news from a cancer standpoint but I'm not sure what it means for treatments and the trial. Trusting God with the plan. thanks for the prayers!!!

Thank you for the update. I will continue to pray.

> Any improvements for Paul and the knee?

Just saw knee doctor today. X-rays looked great. Paul is the same.

> Great in the knee.

Father, You are not surprised by what is going on with Cathy and the medical stuff. You have her best in mind. You have her in Your hands. There is no better place for her to be. But You know the hopes of her heart. So I ask in the midst of decisions, Your peace will absorb her. Give them safe travel and a powerful sense of You. In Jesus name. Amen

Lord, in Your mighty goodness, bring Cathy and Mike rest. Rest and complete peace in all they are a part of. Show Cathy a glimpse of You dancing with her. Help her to see the beauty You see in her right now, where she is. Bless her with the assurance that you have her and her healing all under Your control. In Jesus name. Amen

> I am not in the trial. Will restart chemo in the next week or so. Thanks for the prayers!!!

Blessings my friend.

Father, thank You for Your protection and guidance in the medical decisions made in Cathy's life. Though they weren't what was hoped for, we know You are in control. Be with Cathy and Mike as they navigate this disappointment. Strengthen them in the next steps to come. As always God, we rest in You. Thank You. Bless Cathy with rest today. In Jesus name. Amen

Father, thank You for Your exceedingly, great gift of another day to worship You. Thank You for the rest and peace that reigns over and in Cathy. Continue to bless her as she fully rests in You. In Jesus. Amen.

Lord, there is nothing that you can't do. We place our trust in You for Cathy's healing. You know what is best for her. You want what is best for her. We get confused here about what that is or might be and think only in our narrow way. Forgive us for limiting You. With open hands we surrender our ideas of how things will or should go. We are now ready to take into our emptied hands more of you and your way. Thank You. Bless Cathy today with the peace that comes with surrender. In Jesus name. Amen.

> Amen! So appropriate my friend!

I think I prayed that as much for me as for you my dear friend

> I was thinking that and will do the same. Have you started your book yet? Prayers for My Friend

> You have it already written!

Not written anymore though. Phone ate all my text messages a couple of weeks ago...HA. guess God didn't want me puffing up myself

> Maybe I can get the texts. You would not be puffing yourself up. You can write under a pseudo-name. It puffs up the people that receive the prayers. Your prayers are incredibly encouraging! You could donate some of the proceeds to cancer research. Or headache research

Good idea

Father Your protection is the strongest. As Cathy rests under the wings of Your protection, guide her heart and mind to match your heart and mind.
Send her sweet whispers of Your love today and help her to be aware of them. In Jesus name. Amen.

> Hi there, I did not have chemo yet. My oncologist thinks it is too harsh for me and my white blood cell counts are quite low. She's looking into other options like radiation and she's going to call the MSK doctor. She said she wants me to run the marathon and she's afraid this chemo will shorten that. She said I don't have any cancer below my neck. She's trying to figure out how to treat my neck by itself and keep monitoring the brain. We are just waiting for her to get back in touch with us to find out the next step.

Lord, thank You for the wisdom You give doctors. Thank You for the right treatment that you are working out for Cathy. As these are working out according to your plans give Cathy time to rest and strengthen. Continue to bless and guide her. Continue to rain down Your peace on her. In Jesus name. Amen

Father, You reign Supreme. Nothing can change that. You are working amazing things all around us and in us. Thank You. Continue to walk this path with Cathy. Continue to open the lives around her to your love as she extends it wherever she goes. Lord I ask that you give Cathy overwhelming peace today. Flood her mind, body, and soul with peace. Let nothing shake that peace as she walks this difficult way of healing. Give the medical people the wisdom and knowledge they need in her treatment plan. Thank You for all you are doing. In Jesus name. Amen

> Beautiful prayer Tammie back at you sister! I am looking into downloading these texts but it looks like I have to do it one at a time. I am going to call Verizon or AppleCare and find out if there is an easier way. I still think this would make an awesome book.

Well, now you know that this had to end somewhere, didn't you? And what a better place than at the texts that pushed me to do it in the first place. Though the prayers and texts end here on these pages, the texts continue between Cathy and I, and will until either of us go Home.

Yes, Cathy still has cancer. She hasn't been given a healing just yet. She still faces treatments and drugs and trying to get into new trials to help her stop the cancer. But Cathy is assured of her ultimate healing and carries Jesus in her heart. She shares His love with everyone she encounters. She is a blessing to those of us who know and love her.

So, Cathy, keep holding on strong. Keep believing. I will keep praying and texting.

Blessings,

Tammie

CPSIA information can be obtained
at www.ICGtesting.com
Printed in the USA
BVHW012313070622
639032BV00002B/19